I0017682

Artificial Intelligence
for
Business Leaders

Transform your business with AI and ML

||ARTIFICIAL INTELLIGENCE & MACHINE LEARNING BOOK FOR MANAGERS, LEADERS || ZERO CODING WITH SIMPLE EXPLANATION || LEARN STRATEGY BEHIND AI IMPLEMENTATION || NO PRIOR AI & ML KNOWLEDGE IS REQUIRED ||

Ajit K Jha

Artificial Intelligence for Business Leaders

Copyright © 2020 by Ajit K Jha

All rights reserved. No part of this book may be reproduced in any form without permission in writing from the author.

No part of this publication may be reproduced or transmitted in any form or by any means, mechanical or electronic, including photocopying or recording, or by any information storage and retrieval system, or transmitted by email or by any other means whatsoever without permission in writing from the author.

Disclaimer

Every effort has been made in the preparation of this book to ensure the accuracy of the information presented. However, the information contained in this book is sold without warranty, either express or implied. Neither the author nor publisher or its dealers and distributors will be held liable for any damages caused or alleged to have been caused directly or indirectly by this book. No warranty may be created or extended by sales or promotional materials. The advice and recipes contained herein may not be suitable for everyone.

The fact that an individual, organization of the website is referred to in this work as a citation and/or potential source of further information does not mean that the author endorses the information the individual, organization to the website may provide or recommendations they/it may make. Further, readers should be aware that Internet websites listed in this work might have changed or disappeared between when this work was written and when it is read.

Adherence to all applicable laws and regulations, including international, federal, state, and local governing professional licensing, business practices, advertising, and all other aspects of doing business in any jurisdiction in the world, is the sole responsibility of the purchaser or reader.

ISBN: 9798668732227
Imprint: Independently published

How to best use this book?

The book has been written for business leaders and managers globally with no prior knowledge of artificial intelligence and its other sub-fields. But who wants to incorporate AI in their business practices to achieve not only the desired goals but also gain an edge over their competitors.

The book is a ready reckoner for all the business professionals, analysts, managers, and C-suites globally with its simple explanation of all the key concepts of AI and machine learning and the use cases to help you better understand the positive effects of implementing AI in your regular business practices.

It is recommended to read the book end-to-end to understand the important concepts of this disruptive technology. Understand the subtle differences between AI and machine learning and how a business leader could incorporate in their business practices to achieve greater success.

Please note: All brand names and product names used in this book are trademarks, registered trademarks, or trade names of their respective holders.

Preface

Artificial intelligence (AI) had been making waves in the IT industry since the last decade. It has disrupted the businesses world-over, bringing in changes that were either not perceived earlier or were considered impossible.

Whoever would have thought about chatbots in the recruitment process or self-driven cars to become a reality? While the advances in the field of AI have been exponential, there has been a steady rise in the fear among the professionals. The fear of job loss or being overhauled by AI-enabled bots and humanoids runs strongly amid the professionals and the business leaders globally. Artificial intelligence has opened the door for numerous possibilities, and automation of repetitive and mundane business tasks is just one aspect of it. With AI-enabled tools and technologies, business leaders could spearhead their businesses to unimaginable success.

The technologists are already swearing by the advantages of AI and machine learning (a subset of artificial intelligence), it is time business leaders also understand its importance and incorporate it in their business practices and develop AI-strategies to ensure wholesome success.

The book **Artificial Intelligence for Business Leaders** has been written to serve business leaders globally. With an objective to help you nourish, expand, and enrich your conceptual understanding of all the important aspects of artificial intelligence, and machine learning. The book introduces the readers to AI use-cases, theoretical as well as practical aspects and framework of AI-enabled technology. The book would help you understand how artificial intelligence-enabled tools and technologies are being deployed along with practical aspects of AI technology. The book, with its detailed coverage of all the key topics related to artificial intelligence and machine learning, could help you become an AI expert.

Various advances in the field of artificial intelligence and machine learning have business leaders and managers sit up and take notice of this disruptive technology and what to implement it in their regular business practices to get the desired results at a reduced cost and higher speed.

This book covers all the basic knowledge every business leader should possess before they plan to implement an AI strategy in their business practices. With zero coding and simple explanations, the business leaders and managers globally would be able to use this book to understand not only the concepts of AI but also the application of AI strategy according to their business needs and goals. No prior knowledge of AI or machine learning is recommended or required to read and understand this book.

Acknowledgments

Writing and compiling this book was the hardest part, and that doesn't count the amount of research that I put into it. The toughest part was to keep the language simple so that the intended audience could understand without getting hassled by the technical terms that form the part of this type of assignment.

However, now that I have successfully managed to complete this book as per the best of my abilities and intentions to keep it as simple as possible, it is time for me to pen down my sincere thanks to all the wonderful people who were a part of this journey.

I would also like to thank my friends in the industry for sharing their insights and knowledge with me that helped me in writing this book in a simpler language. I would also like to thank my wife, Vinita Jha, who always kept me motivated through the dark times and despair.

I hope you would enjoy reading the book as much as I enjoyed writing and compiling it.

Table of Contents

Chapter 3 _____ 87

Cognitive Artificial Intelligence 87

Chapter 4 _____ 119

Enterprise AI Strategy _____ 119

Chapter 5 _____ 142

The AI Economy Strategy _____ 142

Chapter 6 _____ 164

AI Success & Failure _____ 164

Chapter 7 _____ 176

Disruption through AI _____ 176

Chapter 10 _____ 223
The Future of AI _____ 223

Chapter 1

Artificial Intelligence: An outline

****
"AI is a new electricity."
- Andrew Ng

****

Sometimes you may have wondered how a robot can perform complex tasks or how computers can play chess? These may seem complex questions to answer but are, in fact, quite easy once you understand how machines learn and adapt to various problems given to them and provide suitable solutions. Machine learning is a technology used to build intelligent systems. These systems can learn from past experiences or analyze historical data and provide results accordingly.

Machine learning is a branch of artificial intelligence, which is making its presence felt in numerous fields. In robotics, machine learning helps robots to navigate better. In medical science, based on historical data, machine learning can be used to predict the best treatment for a disease. Speech recognition is another example of machine learning technology wherein systems identify your voice by learning from your voice patterns.

What Is Machine Learning?

Machine learning is the process by which machines learn from experience and use it to improve their performance. Prof. E. Alpaydin defines machine learning as "Optimizing a performance criterion using example data and experience."

Data is a critical element in machine learning. Machine learning algorithms are applied to data to identify hidden patterns and gain insights. These insights help systems to learn and improve their performance automatically. This technique is especially relevant in the case of big data, wherein organizations can use a massive volume of data to gain insights and make vital predictions such as customer behavior or sales predictions.

Machine learning technology is being used in numerous areas such as artificial neural networks, voice recognition, facial patterns, data mining, web ranking, and many more. Most of us use machine learning technology without being aware of it. One of the most common uses of this technology is in the identification of spam or junk email. A spam filtering tool, SpamAssassin, has been developed with the help of machine learning technology. Snapchat's filters use augmented reality and machine learning for the flower crown's selfies.

"Machine Learning is a subset of the Artificial Intelligence (AI) technique, which uses statistical methods to enable machines to improve with experience."
Or
"Machine Learning is a kind of Artificial Intelligence (AI) that provides computers the ability to learn without being explicitly programmed."

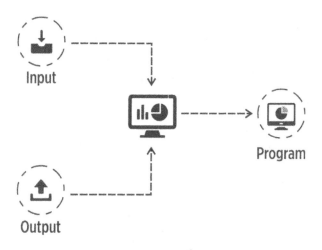

How does machine learning work?

Each flavor of machine learning and each model works in different ways, exploiting different parts of mathematics and data science. However, in general, machine learning works by taking in data, finding relationships within the data, and giving us output what the model learned, as illustrated in the following diagram:

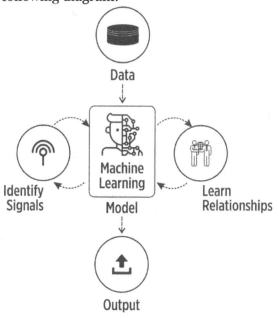

As you explore the different types of machine learning models, you will see how they manipulate data differently and come up with various outputs for different applications.

Use Case: - Diabetes diagnosis

Patient: I want to get diagnosed for diabetes
Doctor: Ok let me check the reports

no._ of times	glucose_ conc	blood_ pressure	skin_fold_ thickness	2-hour_serum _insulin	BMI	diabetes	age
6	148	72	35	0	33.6	0.627	50

→ Doctor → Diabetic (Y/N)

After analyzing the patient's report, the doctor, with the help of his experience, can diagnose whether the patient has diabetes or not.

You would now want to train a machine to do the doctor's task. For this purpose, you would need to train the machine with the same experience/knowledge using historical data of more than 50 thousand patients.

no._ of _times	glucose _conc	blood _pressure	skin_fold _thickness	2-hour _serum_insulin	BMI	diabetes	age	is_ diabetic
6	148	72	35	0	33.6	0.627	50	Yes
1	85	66	29	0	26.6	0.351	31	No
8	183	64	0	0	23.3	0.672	32	Yes
1	89	66	23	94	28.1	0.167	21	No
0	137	40	35	168	43.1	2.2888	33	Yes
5	116	74	0	0	25.6	0.201	30	No
3	78	50	32	88	31	0.248	26	Yes
10	115	0	0	0	35.3	0.131	29	No
2	197	70	45	543	30.5	0.158	53	Yes
8	125	96	0	0	0	0.232	54	Yes
4	110	92	0	0	37.6	0.191	30	No
10	168	74	0	0	38	0.537	34	Yes
10	139	80	0	0	27.1	1.441	57	No
1	189	60	23	846	30.1	0.398	59	Yes
5	166	72	19	175	25.8	0.587	51	Yes

→ Diabetic

Non Diabetic

Characteristics

The problem has the following characteristics:
1. Labeled learning data and output is available.

2. You have historical data, using which machine can find the relationship between the input and the output
3. Output classes are predefined. i.e., diabetic, or not diabetic

Flow Graph –

After learning from the training data, the machine will create specific rules/models, as depicted by this flow chart.

Classifying New Data Input

no._of _times	glucose _conc	blood_ pressure	skin_fold_ thickness	2-hour_ serum_insulin	BMI	diabetes	age
8	183	64	0	0	23.3	0.672	32

Input   Model   Output

Based on the model created from the training data, the machine is now able to classify into predefined classes, which in this case are 'diabetic' or 'not diabetic.'

Machine classifying data into predefined classes is called supervised learning.

Features of Machine Learning

1. It uses the data to detect patterns in a dataset and adjust program actions accordingly.
2. In machine learning, computer programs can teach themselves to grow and change when exposed to new data.
3. It is used to discover hidden insights and enables computers to use iterative algorithms without being explicitly programmed.
4. It automates the analytical model building using statistical data and machine learning algorithms.

Traditional Approach vs. Machine Learning Approach

Traditional Programming: You code the behavior of the program. It relies on hard-coded rules.

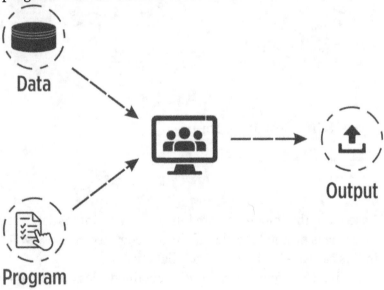

Data

Program

Output

Machine Learning: You feed the data once, and then based on that data, the machine continues to learn.

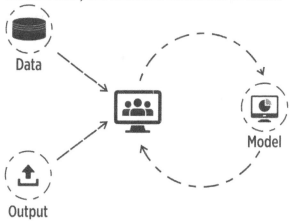

Machine Learning Types

There are numerous ways to segment machine learning and dive deeper. One can segment machine learning models by different characteristics like:

- The types of data/organic structures they utilize (tree/graph/neural network)
- The field of mathematics they are most related to (statistical/probabilistic)
- The level of computation required to train (deep learning)

For understanding, let's divide machine learning models into the following three subsets:

- Supervised learning
- Unsupervised learning
- Reinforcement learning

Applications of Machine Learning

You learned about SpamAssassin and how it filters spam emails. While SpamAssassin uses machine learning technology to filter emails, the list below denotes some of the many areas where machine learning is used:

- Speech Recognition
- Image Recognition
- Medical Diagnosis
- Statistical Arbitrage
- Learning Associations
- Classification
- Prediction
- Extraction
- Regression

The following are the details of machine learning applications at a broad level, and we will also discuss in detail in the later part of the book.

Speech Recognition (SR)

Speech Recognition is the ability of a machine or program to convert the spoken words into text. It allows humans to use their voices to communicate with software. It is also known as "computer speech recognition," "automatic speech recognition (ASR)," or "speech to text (STT)." The dimensions in this machine learning application might be a set of numbers that represent the speech signals. You can segment the signal into portions that contain distinct phonemes or words. In each segment, you can describe the speech signal by the intensities or energy in different time-frequency bands. It can also use simple data, structured documents, speech-to-text processing.

Image Recognition (IR)

Image Recognition is the most common use of machine learning. In many circumstances, wherein the object is being classified as a digital image, it recognizes objects, places, people, and actions in an image. The measurements, in this case, might describe the outputs of each pixel in the image.

Medical Diagnosis (MD)

ML provides methods, tools, and techniques that can help in solving diagnostic and prognostic challenges in many medical domains. It is used for the analysis of clinical parameters and their combinations for prognosis, e.g., extraction of medical knowledge, prediction of disease progression for outcomes research, therapy planning and support, and patient management. Machine learning is being used for data analysis, such as interpretation of continuous data, detection of regularities in the data used in the Intensive Care Unit, and intelligent alarming for effective and efficient monitoring. ML methods, once implemented successfully, can help to integrate computer-based systems in the healthcare environment to provide opportunities to enable and enhance the work of medical experts and eventually improving the effectiveness and quality of medical care.

In medical diagnosis, the foremost interest is in establishing the presence of a disease, which is followed by its precise identification wherein a separate category for each disease is considered, and one category is kept for the cases where no condition is present. At this point, machine learning improves the accuracy of medical diagnosis by investigating the data of patients.

The measurements in machine learning applications are typically the results of specific medical tests (example various blood tests, blood pressure, and temperature) or medical diagnostics (such as medical images), presence/absence/intensity of multiple symptoms and necessary physical information about the patient (age, sex, weight, etc.). The doctors narrow down on the disease wreaking the patient based on the results of the above measurements.

Statistical Arbitrage

In finance, statistical arbitrage refers to automated trading strategies that are short-term and involve a large number of securities. Users try to implement trading algorithms for a group of securities based on parameters such as historical correlation and general economic variables. These measurements can be used as a classification or estimation problem. The underlying assumption is that prices will move toward a historical average.

You apply machine learning methods to obtain index arbitrage strategies. In particular, you apply linear regression and support vector regression (SVR) to the prices of exchange-traded funds and a range of stocks. By using principal component analysis (PCA) to reduce the dimensionality of the feature space, you observe the benefits and notice the problems in SVR applications.

In the case of classification, the categories may be to sell, buy, or do nothing for each security. To arrive at an estimate, you can predict the expected return from each security over a future time horizon. You usually use the forecast of expected earnings to make trading decisions (buy, sell, etc.).

Learning Associations (LA)

Learning associations (LA) is the process of developing insights into various associations between products. A good example is how seemingly irrelevant products might reveal the relationship between each other when analyzing the purchasing behavior of customers.

Machine learning can be used to conduct Market basket analysis (MBA), which is the study of the products that people buy. If a buyer buys 'X,' would he or she be inclined to buy 'Y' because the two products are related? It leads to the relationship that exists between fish and chips. When new products launch in the market, knowing these existing relationships, marketers visualize a new relationship. This understanding can help suggest related products to customers. If the customer has a higher purchasing possibility, it can also help bundle the product for better packaging. Once you find associations by examining a large amount of sales data, big data analysts can formulate rules to derive probability tests when learning conditional probabilities.

Classification

Classification is the process of separating individuals from many categories of research objects. They are called independent variables. Classification helps analysts use the object's metrics to determine the category to which the object belongs. To establish effective rules, analysts use data. The data contains many examples of objects with the correct classification. For instance, before a bank decides to issue a loan, it evaluates the customer's ability to pay. You can do this by considering factors such as customer income, age, savings, and financial history. This information is taken from past data on loans. Analysts establish a relationship between customer attributes and associated risks.

Prediction

Consider the example of a bank that calculates the probability of any loan applicant defaulting the loan. To calculate the possibility of default, the system must first classify the available data into specific groups. It is portrayed by a set of rules prescribed by the analysts. Once you rank according to the need, you can calculate the probability. These probability calculations can be calculated in all sectors for various purposes. The above prediction is one of the best machine learning algorithms. Let's take an example of retail; some time back, we were able to obtain information such as the sales report of last month/year /5 years/ Good Friday/Christmas – this type of report is called a historical report. But currently, companies are more interested in finding out sales that might happen next month/year/Christmas so that the organization can make necessary decisions for procurement, stocks, among other things on time.

Extraction

Information Extraction (IE) is another machine learning application. It is the process of extracting structured information from unstructured data, for example, web pages, articles, blogs, business reports, and emails. The relational database sustains the output produced by the information extraction. The extraction process takes data as a set of documents and produces structured data. This result is in summary forms, such as an Excel sheet and a table in a relational database. Today, mining is becoming a key in the Big Data industry. A massive volume of data is being generated, of which most of the data is unstructured. The first key challenge is managing unstructured data and converting it to a structured pattern so that it can be stored in RDBMS. These days the data collection mechanism is also changing. Earlier, we collected data in batches like at the end of the day (EOD), but now, the company wants the data as soon as it is produced - that is, in real-time.

Regression

You can apply machine learning to regression also. Suppose $m = m_1, m_2, m_3, \ldots m^n$ are the input variables, and y is the output variable. You can utilize machine learning technology to produce the output (y) based on the input variables (m), and you can build a model to express the relationship between various parameters.

$Y = g$ (m), where g a function, depends on the specific characteristics of the model. In regression, you can use the machine learning principle to optimize the parameters, cut the approximation error, and calculate the closest possible result. You can also use machine learning to optimize functions. You can choose to alter the inputs to get a better model. It offers a new and improved model to work with.

Machine Learning Applications in Daily Life
Traffic Alerts (Maps)

Google Maps is undoubtedly THE app you use whenever you go out and require assistance in directions and traffic. You may have traveled to another city and took the expressway, and Maps suggested: "Despite the heavy traffic, you are on the fastest route." But how does it know that?

It is a combination of people currently using the service, historical data of that route collected over time, and some tricks acquired from other companies. Everyone who uses Maps provides their location, average speed, the route they travel, which in turn helps Google collect massive traffic data, making them predict upcoming traffic and adjust the route accordingly.

Self-Driving Cars

This is one of the most refreshing applications of machine learning. Machine learning plays a vital role in driverless cars. Their current artificial intelligence, powered by hardware manufacturer

---

NVIDIA, uses the unsupervised learning algorithm. NVIDIA stated that they did not train their model to detect any object or people as such. The model works on deep learning and brings together data sources from all of its vehicles and its drivers. It uses internal and external sensors that are part of the IoT. According to the data collected by McKinsey, the automotive data will be worth over $1000 Billion in 2025.

Transportation and Commuting

If you've ever used an app to book a taxi, say Uber, you're already using machine learning to some degree. It provides a personalized application that is unique to you, automatically detects your location, and provides options to go to your home or office or any other frequent place based on your history and patterns.

It uses the machine learning algorithm layered on historical trip data to make a more accurate ETA prediction. With machine learning, it has higher accuracy in delivery and pickup. Although you use GPS navigation services, your current locations and speed are stored on a central server to manage traffic. This data is used to build a map of the current traffic. While this helps to prevent traffic flow and does a congestion analysis, the underlying problem is that there are fewer GPS-equipped cars. Machine learning in such scenarios helps to estimate the regions where congestion can be found based-on daily experiences.

Products Recommendations

Imagine, you check an item on Amazon, but you do not buy it then and there. But the next day, you are watching videos on YouTube, and suddenly you see an ad for the same article. You switch to Facebook, and there you also see the same advertisement. So, how does this happen?

You Viewed

PRODUCT A

ADD TO CART

Customers who viewed this also viewed:

PRODUCT B

ADD TO CART

PRODUCT C

ADD TO CART

PRODUCT D

ADD TO CART

Google tracks your search history and recommends ads based on your search history - another interesting application of machine learning. Product recommendations help Amazon to generate more than 35% of its revenue.

Virtual Personal Assistants

Virtual Personal Assistants help you find useful information with text or voice. Some of the many machine learning applications include:

- Speech recognition
- Speech to text conversion
- Natural Language Processing
- Text to speech conversion

Alexa, Cortana, and Siri are some of the popular examples of virtual personal assistants. As their names suggest, they help find information when asked by voice. All you need to do is activate them and ask, "What is my schedule for today?", "What are the flights from New York to Tokyo?" or similar questions. To respond, your assistant searches for the information, remember your related queries or sends a command to other resources (such as phone applications) to collect information. You can even instruct assistants for specific tasks such as "Set an alarm for 6 am the next day," "Remind me to visit the visa office the day after tomorrow." Machine learning is an integral part of these personal assistants, as they collect and refine information based-on your previous involvement with them. Later, this dataset is used to generate results that are tailored to your preferences. Virtual assistants are integrated into a variety of platforms.

For example, Smartphones (iPhone, Samsung, etc.), smart speakers (Google Home, Amazon Echo, etc.), and more.

Dynamic Pricing

Establishing the correct price for a product or service is an old problem in economic theory. There are a large number of pricing strategies that depend on the objective sought. Whether it's a movie ticket, a plane ticket, or taxi fares, everything is dynamically priced. Now, artificial intelligence has allowed pricing solutions to follow purchasing trends and determine more competitive product prices.

When to implement Dynamic Pricing:
1. Based on timing
2. Based on demand
3. Based on demography
4. Based on competitor pricing
5. Based on service time
6. Based on pricing launch
7. Based on bulk orders

Uber's Pricing Strategies

Uber's most important use of machine learning comes in the form of surge pricing, a machine learning model known as "Geosurge". If you're late for a meeting and need to reserve an Uber in a crowded area, be prepared to pay double the standard fare. Same for flights as well, if you are traveling in the holiday season, chances are prices maybe double the original price.

Google Translate

Remember the time you traveled to a new place, and it was difficult for you to communicate with the locals or find local places where everything was written in a different language. Google's GNMT (Google Neural Machine Translation) is an end-to-end learning approach for automated translation that works in thousands of languages and dictionaries, uses Natural Language Processing to provide the most accurate translation of any sentence or words. Since the tone of the words is also essential, use other techniques such as NER (named entity recognition), POS tagging, and many more. It is one of the best-used machine learning applications.

Online Video Streaming (Netflix)

With over 100 million subscribers, Netflix is undoubtedly the leader in the online streaming world. The rapid rise of Netflix has surprised all film industry people-forcing them to ask: "Which website can succeed in Hollywood?" The answer is Netflix, which uses machine learning extensively. The Netflix algorithm continuously collects large amounts of data about user activity, such as:

- At what point you paused, replayed, or fast-forwarded the content.
- On which specific day you watched the content (TV shows on weekdays and movies on weekends).
- When you returned and left the content (if you come back again)?
- What rating did you give? (Netflix receives about 4 million ratings and 3 million search queries per day).
- How did you browse and scroll? And many more details like that.

Once the Netflix algorithm collects this kind of data for each subscriber, it uses many machine learning applications 'for recommendation systems. Therefore, they have such a high customer retention rate.

Social Media Services

Social media platforms are using machine learning to benefit themselves and users, from personalizing your news sources for better advertising positions. One of the most widely used applications of machine learning is automatic friend tagging suggestions on Facebook or any other social media platform. Facebook uses face detection and recognition to automatically find the person's face and match it in the database and suggest that you tag the person according to DeepFace. Facebook's deep learning project named DeepFace is responsible for recognizing faces and identifying people in pictures. It also provides Alt tags (alternative tags) for images that have been uploaded to Facebook. E.g., if you inspect the image on Facebook, the alt-tag has a description. Continuous learning suggests a list of Facebook users that you can become friends with.

Similar Pins: Machine learning is the principal element of Computer Vision, which is a technique to extract useful information from images and videos. Pinterest uses computer vision to identify the objects (or pins) in the images and recommend similar pins accordingly.

Email Spam and Malware Filtering

Email clients use several spam filters. Machine learning is used to ascertain that these spam filters are continuously updated. After completing rule-based spam filtering, it cannot track the latest techniques used by spammers. Multi-Layer Perceptron, Decision Tree Induction are some of the spam filtering techniques that are powered by ML.

More than 325,000 malware are detected every day, and each code segment is similar to the previous version. The system security program supported by machine learning can understand the coding pattern. Therefore, they easily detect new malware with a 2–10% variation and offer protection against them.

Search Engine Result Refining

Search engines like Google and others use machine learning to improve your search results. Every time you perform a search, the back-end algorithm monitors how you respond to the results. If you open the top result and stay on the page for a long time, the search engine will assume that it displays the results according to the query. In the same way, if you reach the second or third page of search results, but do not open any results, the search engine estimates that the results provided do not meet the requirements. In this way, the back-end algorithm can improve search results.

Online Fraud Detection

Machine learning is making cyberspace a secure place; tracking monetary frauds online is one example. PayPal is using ML to prevent money laundering. The company uses several tools to help them compare the millions of transactions that occur and distinguish between legal and illegal transactions between buyers and sellers.

Experts predict that online credit card fraud will soar to $40 billion in 2022. This exceeds the combined profits of Coca-Cola and JP Morgan Chase. Fraud detection is one of the essential applications of machine learning. The increase in the number of transactions is due to numerous payment channels-credit/debit cards, smartphones, various wallets, UPI, etc. At the same time, many criminals are already good at finding loopholes.

Whenever a customer makes a transaction, the machine learning model will thoroughly scan for suspicious patterns in their data. In machine learning, problems such as fraud detection are often classified as classification problems.

What is Artificial Intelligence (AI)?

Artificial Intelligence is a way of making machines think and behave intelligently. These machines are controlled by software within them, so AI has a lot to do with smart software

---

programs that control these machines. It is a science to find theories and methodologies that can help machines understand the world and, consequently, react to situations in the same way that humans do. If you look closely at how the AI field has emerged in recent decades, you will see that many researchers tend to focus on different concepts to define AI. In the modern world, AI is used in many verticals in many different ways. You would want machines to detect, think, reason, and act and also want your machines to be rational. AI is closely connected to the study of the human brain. The researchers believe that AI can be achieved by understanding how the human mind works.

By mirroring the way, the human brain learns, thinks, and acts, you can build a machine that can do the same. AI can be used as a platform to develop intelligent systems with learning capacity. According to the dictionary, "artificial intelligence is the ability of a machine to imitate human behavior." It allows computers to imitate human intelligence using logic. A machine with the ability to achieve cognitive functions such as perceiving, reasoning, learning, and solving problems is an artificial intelligence machine. The target for AI is the human level of thought, speech, and vision.

Stages of AI

1. Artificial Narrow Intelligence (ANI): The most common form of AI you would find in the market is ANI. These Artificial Intelligence systems are intended to solve a single problem and could perform a single task well. They have limited capabilities, such as recommending a product for an e-commerce user or predicting the weather. This is the only type of Artificial Intelligence that exists today. They can approach human functioning in particular contexts and even exceed them in many cases, but they only excel in highly controlled environments with a limited set of parameters. Examples of ANI: Smartphone apps, Chess and AlphaGo, image identification tools, speech recognition tools, self-driving systems, Google Translate, spam filters, etc.

2. Artificial General Intelligence (AGI): An artificial intelligence reaches the general state wherein it can perform any intellectual task with the same level of precision as a human. It is defined as AI, which has a cognitive function at the human level in a wide variety of domains, for instance, image processing, language processing, computational functioning, and reasoning. You are still far behind building an AGI system, and this is still a theoretical concept. An AGI system would need to comprise thousands of Narrow Artificial Intelligence systems working together and communicating with each other to imitate human reasoning. Even with the most advanced infrastructure and computer systems, like IBM's Watson, it has taken 40 minutes to simulate a single second of neural activity. This gives you vital information about the interconnectedness and high complexity of the human brain, and about the extent of challenges you would face while building an AI with your existing resources. A perfect AI will be able to integrate multipurpose systems and will be able to drive them with human-level intelligence (reasoning, thinking, and decision-making). It will be able to analyze diverse information and make decisions accordingly.

3. Artificial Super Intelligence (ASI): An AI is super when it can beat humans in many tasks. In other words, machines are smarter than humans or surpass human intelligence. It would include making rational decisions and functions, like creating better art and building emotional relationships. Examples. Super Intelligent AI agents, systems that are masters at every skill, subject, or discipline and are faster than the smartest humans.

Three Stages of AI: At a Glance

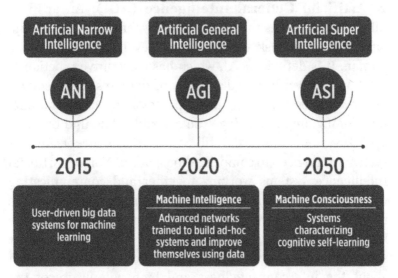

Three Stages of AI: At a Glance

Artificial Narrow Intelligence	Artificial General Intelligence	Artificial Super Intelligence
ANI	AGI	ASI
2015	2020	2050
User-driven big data systems for machine learning	**Machine Intelligence** Advanced networks trained to build ad-hoc systems and improve themselves using data	**Machine Consciousness** Systems characterizing cognitive self-learning

Why Artificial Intelligence?

AI can affect all aspects of our lives. The AI field tries to understand the patterns and behaviors of entities. With AI, you would not only want to build intelligent systems but also understand the concept of intelligence. The smart systems that are made are extremely helpful in understanding how an intelligent system like your brain creates another intelligent system. Unlike other fields like mathematics or physics that have been around for centuries, AI is still in its infancy. In the past few decades, AI has produced some spectacular products, such as autonomous cars and smart robots that can walk. Based on the direction where the world is heading, it is quite evident that gaining intelligence will have a significant impact on humans for years to come.

You can't resist the urge to think about how the human mind figures out how to accomplish such a great deal without any problem. You can perceive objects, get dialects, learn new things, and perform a lot progressively refined assignments with your minds. How does the human mind do this? At the point when you attempt to do these activities with a machine, you will see it falls behind. For example, when you try to search for things like extra-terrestrial life or time travel, you don't know if those things exist. The good thing about AI's holy grail is that you know it exists. Your brain is the holy grail! It is a spectacular illustration of an intelligent system. All you have to do is imitate its functionality to create an intelligent system that can do something similar, possibly even more.

These days, artificial intelligence is used in almost every industry, giving a technological advantage to all companies that integrate artificial intelligence at scale. According to McKinsey, artificial intelligence has the potential to create USD 600 billion in retail, providing 50 percent more incremental value in banking compared to other analytical techniques. In transportation and logistics, the potential revenue increase is 89 percent or more. Specifically, if an organization uses artificial intelligence for its marketing team, it can automate routine and monotonous tasks, allowing the sales representative to focus on tasks such as building relationships, raising leads, etc. A "Gong" company provides a conversation intelligence service. Every time a sales representative makes a phone call, the machine records transcripts and analyzes the chat. The VP can use AI analysis and recommendations to formulate a winning strategy.

In a nutshell, AI provides cutting-edge technology to handle complex data, which is impossible for a human to manage. AI automates redundant jobs, allowing workers to focus on high-level, essential tasks. When AI is applied at scale, it leads to reduced costs and increases revenue.

Let's see how raw data is converted to wisdom through various levels of processing:

One of the foremost reasons everyone wants to study AI is to automate many tasks. In the present world, organizations handle massive and impossible amounts of data. The human brain cannot track that much data.

The data originates from multiple sources simultaneously and is disorganized and chaotic. The knowledge derived from this data must be continually updated as the data itself changes continuously. The sensing and analysis must happen in real-time with high precision.

Although the human brain is excellent at analyzing things around it, but it cannot keep up with other conditions such as to store a large amount of information, make decisions in adverse conditions, etc. Therefore, there is a need to design and develop smart machines, which can store a massive amount of data. There is a need for artificial intelligence systems that can efficiently handle large amounts of data.

With the advent of Cloud Computing, the organizations can now:

- Store massive amounts of data,
- Ingest data simultaneously from multiple sources without delay,
- Index and organize data in a way that allows us to derive insights.
- Learn from new data and update continuously using the correct learning algorithms.
- Think and respond to situations based on real-time conditions.

AI techniques are being actively used to make existing machines smarter so they can execute tasks faster and more efficiently.

Applications of Artificial Intelligence

Artificial Intelligence in Practice

Google's AlphaGo: A computer program that plays the  board game, "Go." It is the first computer program to defeat a human "Go" world champion.

Amazon's Alexa: A home controlled AI-based device that responds to humans speaking to it.

IBM Watson: IBM  Watson is a computer system that can answer your questions. It is based on cognitive computing. Cognitive computing is a combination of natural language processing, machine learning, artificial intelligence, reasoning, and other technologies.

Concierge robot from IBM Watson

Branches of AI Understanding the various fields of study within AI is essential so that the right framework can be chosen to solve real-world problems. Here is a list of key topics:

Machine learning and pattern recognition: - This is perhaps the most prevalent form of AI. A software system is designed and developed that can learn from data. Based on these learning models, you make predictions about unknown data. One of the main limitations here is that these programs are limited to the power of the data. If the data set is small, the learning models would also be defined.

Let's see what a unique machine learning system looks like:

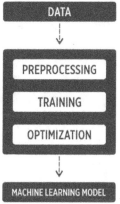

When a system makes an observation, it compares it to what it has already seen as a pattern. For example, in a facial recognition system, the software will try to match the pattern of eyes, nose, lips, eyebrows, etc. to find a face in the existing user database.

Logic-based AI: Mathematical logic is used to run computer programs in logic-based AI. A logic-based AI program is a set of statements in a logical form that expresses facts and rules about a problem domain. It is widely used in pattern matching, language analysis, and semantic analysis, etc.

Search: Search techniques are widely used in AI programs. These programs study a large number of possibilities and then choose the most optimal path. For example, this is commonly used in strategy games such as chess, networking, resource allocation, and programming, etc.

Representation of knowledge: The facts about the world must be represented in some way for a system to make sense. The languages of mathematical logic are recurrently used here. If knowledge is represented proficiently, systems can keep growing smarter.

Ontology is a related field of study that deals with the types of objects that exist. It is a formal description of the properties and relationships of entities that exist in a domain. This is

---

generally done with a specific taxonomy or hierarchical structure or something to that effect.

The following diagram shows the difference between information and knowledge:

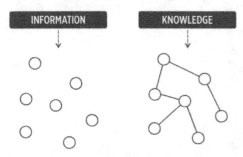

Planning: Planning gives us maximum returns with minimum costs. These software programs begin with facts about the situation and a statement of a goal. These programs are also aware of the facts of the world, so they know what the rules are. From this information, they generate the most optimal plan to achieve the objective of the goal.

Heuristics: A heuristic is a technique used to solve a practical problem. It is useful for solving the problem in the short term, but it is not guaranteed to be optimal. This is more like an educated guess about what approach you should take to solve a problem. In AI, you would frequently encounter situations wherein you cannot check every single possibility to pick the best option. Therefore, you must use heuristics to achieve the objective. They are widely used in AI in fields like robotics, and search engines, etc.

Genetic programming: Genetic programming is a way of making programs to solve a task, matching programs, and selecting the most suitable one. The programs are coded as a set of genes, using an algorithm to obtain a program that can perform the given task well.

Statistics and data mining

- **Statistics** is the discipline concerned with the assortment, analysis, explanation, representation, and drawing of inductions from the information. Its emphasis is on depicting the properties of a dataset and the connections that exist between information. Statistics usually are not considered as a part of AI. However, numerous methods do structure the facility for or use related AI procedures.

- **Descriptive statistics** depict or envisions the essential highlights of the information being examined. A simple application could be to locate a best-selling retail item in a store in a period.

- **Inferential statistics** are utilized to make determinations that apply to something beyond the information being considered. This is important when investigation must be conducted on a smaller, representative dataset when the actual population is excessively huge or hard to consider. As the analysis is performed on a subset of the total data, the inferences that can be achieved with inferential statistics are never 100 percent accurate, and instead are just probabilistic bets. Electoral surveys, for example, are based on surveying a small percentage of citizens to assess the feelings of the entire population as you saw during the 2016 US electoral cycle. In the USA, the conclusions drawn from the samples may not reflect reality.

- **Data mining** is the automation of exploratory statistical analysis for large-scale databases. However, the term is frequently used to depict any sort of algorithmic information investigation and data preparation, which may likewise incorporate AI and deep learning strategies. The objective of data mining is to extract patterns and information from large-scale

---

datasets with the goal that they can be reshaped into a more logical structure for later investigation.

Symbolic and expert systems

- Symbol system is a program that uses human-understandable symbols to express problems and reasoning. The most successful form of the symbol system is the expert system, which imitates the decision-making process of human experts. The expert system has a series of production rules, like if-then statements, which control how programs access the knowledge base and make inferences.

- Rule-based expert systems are of utmost effectiveness when applied to automatic calculations and logic processes wherein rules and results are relatively clear. As decisions become more complex or nuanced, it becomes impossible to standardize all the necessary knowledge and reasoning schemes needed to make human-level decisions.

- The rules engine and knowledge base for an expert system must be hand-engineered by domain experts. It is a significant disadvantage due to the limited number of experts who can perform tasks and the extra time required to program such complex systems. The "comprehensiveness" of the knowledge base is questionable. It will require continuous maintenance (another considerable disadvantage, that involves a lot of expenditure), and the accuracy of the system is too dependent on the possibility of wrong expert opinion. Although symbol systems are historically neither scalable nor adaptable, recent research has investigated them, combining them with newer methods such as machine learning and deep learning to improve performance.

Chapter **2**

The Artificial Intelligence Gamut

****

"We are now solving the problems of machine learning and artificial intelligence in the realm of science fiction over the past few decades."

- Jeff Bezos, Amazon

****

Artificial intelligence, Machine learning, and Deep learning Artificial intelligence can be divided into three sub-fields:

- **Artificial Intelligence (AI):**
  The theory and development of computer systems to be able to perform tasks that usually require human intelligence. Al and ML are used interchangeably frequently, but they are not the same. ML is one of the most active areas and a way to achieve Al. Al is the science of pattern recognition and mimicking human behavior.

  Al powered computers have started simulating the human brain work styles, sensations, actions, interactions, perceptions, and cognitive abilities. However, all these developments are either at the primary or intermediate level. Once, it was believed that human intelligence could be precisely described, and machines can simulate it with Al.

- **Machine Learning (ML):**

  A field of computer science that uses statistical techniques to give computer systems the ability to "learn" (e.g., progressively improve performance on a specific task) with data, without being explicitly programmed. ML is a subset of AI and an approach to achieve AI. Neural networks are an essential component of AI; what you simply need is MLaaS (Machine Learning as a Service) for everyone.

- **Deep Learning (DL):**

  It is also known as hierarchical learning or deep structured learning. Deep learning is a part of a broader family of machine learning methods based on learning data representations, as opposed to task-specific algorithms. DL is a subset of machine learning, or in other words, it is a technique for implementing potent and superior machine learning. The objective of the methods is to achieve a goal or an artificial intelligence power that teaches computers to do tasks and gain the ability to understand anything.

  "Deep learning is an algorithm that has no theoretical limitations of what it can learn; the more data you give, and the more computational time you provide, the better it is." Sir Geoffrey Hinton

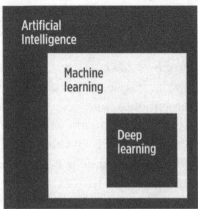

The three concentric levels above describe DL as a subset of ML, which is a subset of AI. Therefore, AI is the all-encompassing concept wherein the other two concepts are rooted. ML thrived later, and now DL is promising to advance AI to another level.

Artificial Intelligence vs. Machine Learning vs. Data Science

Artificial Intelligence, much like data science, is a wide field of applications, systems, and more that aims at replicating human intelligence through machines. Artificial Intelligence represents action-planned feedback for perception.

Perception > Planning > Action > Feedback of Perception

Data science uses different parts of this loop to solve specific problems. For example, in the first step (that is, perception), data scientists try to use data to identify patterns. Similarly, in the next step (i.e., planning), they try to:

- find all possible solutions
- find the best solution

After planning, the next step is action, and so on. Data Science creates a system that interrelates both the above points and helps businesses move forward. Data Science isn't precisely a subset of machine learning, but it uses ML to analyze data and make predictions. It integrates ML with other disciplines, like big data analytics and cloud computing. Data Science completely focuses on real-world problems and is a practical application of ML.

Even though the terms Artificial Intelligence (AI), Machine Learning (ML), and Data Science (DS) follow in the same domain and are connected, but they have their specific applications and meaning.

Artificial Intelligence systems mimic or replicate human intelligence. ML gives the systems the ability to learn and improve from experiences without performing them. Data science is an umbrella term that incorporates data analytics, data mining, machine learning, artificial intelligence, and other several related disciplines. The below infographic explains the relationship between AI, ML, and DS.

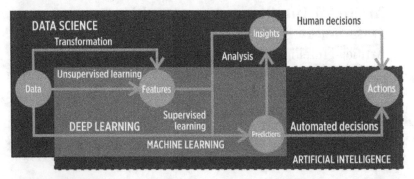

	Artificial Intelligence (AI)	Machine Learning (ML)	Data Science (DS)
How does it work?	AI combines large amounts of data through iterative processing and intelligent algorithms to help computers learn automatically	ML uses efficient programs that can use data to self-learn without having to be instructed explicitly	DS works by sourcing, cleaning, and processing data to extract meaning out of it for analytical purposes
Tools Used	• TensorFlow • Scikit Learn • Keras	• Amazon Lex • Scikit Learn • IBM Watson Studio • Microsoft Azure ML Studio	• SAS • Tableau • Apache Spark • MATLAB • BigML
Applications	• Chatbots • Voice Assistant • Healthcare	• Autonomous driving • Recommendation System • Facial recognition	• Healthcare analysis • Fraud & Risk detection • Ecommerce

Artificial Intelligence (AI) vs. Machine Learning (ML)

Most of your smartphones, everyday devices, and even the Internet use artificial intelligence. Large companies that want to announce their latest innovations often use AI and machine learning interchangeably, though machine learning and AI are different in some ways.

Artificial Intelligence is a computer with human-like characteristics. Grab your brain; it can easily and seamlessly calculate the world around us. A computer can accomplish the same job through artificial intelligence. Artificial Intelligence is a broad science that mimics the human ability to create intelligent machines.

ML (a subset of AI) refers to systems that can learn from experience. Machine learning models look for patterns in the data and then try to draw conclusions. In a nutshell, there is no need to program the machine manually. The programmer gives some examples from which the computer learns how to adapt.

Machine Learning (ML) vs. Data Science (DS)

Data Science and Machine Learning are closely related. Data Science helps to evaluate the data of machine learning algorithms. Data Science covers the entire range of data processing and machine learning in terms of algorithms or statistics aspects.

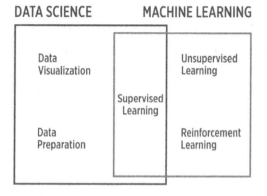

DATA SCIENCE   MACHINE LEARNING

Data Visualization	Supervised Learning	Unsupervised Learning
Data Preparation		Reinforcement Learning

- Data science is the use of statistical methods to find patterns in the data.
- Data science includes techniques like statistical modeling, visualization, and pattern recognition.
- Machine learning focuses on developing algorithms from the data provided.
- Machine learning practices similar kinds of techniques as data science.

Machine Learning Techniques

Classification: Separating into groups having definite values, e.g., 0 or 1, cat or dog, orange, or apple, etc. It is used to classify new observations, predict discrete responses, and predict qualitative targets.

Categorization: This is a technique to organize data into categories for its most effective and efficient use.

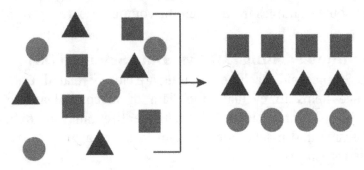

Clustering: Cluster analysis or clustering is the task of grouping a group of objects so that objects in the same group are more similar to each other (in a sense) than the objects in other groups. Clustering is a method of unsupervised learning and is a common technique used for statistical data analysis in many fields.

CLUSTERING

PRE-CLUSTERING	POST-CLUSTERING

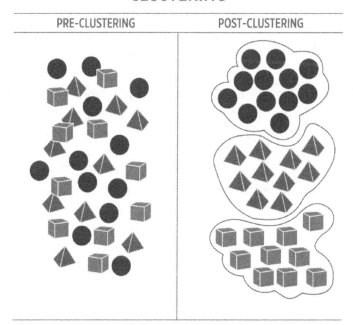

Trend Analysis: Represents variations of low frequency in a time series; the high and medium frequency fluctuations being out.

Anomaly Detection: This is a technique of identifying rare events or observations, which can raise suspicions by being statistically different from the rest of the observations. Such "anomalous" behavior typically translates to some kind of a problem like a credit card fraud, machine failure in a server, a cyber-attack, etc.

Data Visualization: Data visualization creates patterns or images from data by using algorithms so that users can effectively understand and respond to the data.

Decision Tree: A decision tree is a decision support instrument that uses a tree-like decision model and its likely consequences, including chance event outcomes, resource costs, and utility. This is a method of displaying algorithms that contain only conditional control statements. Decision trees are commonly used in operational research, especially in decision analysis. They help in identifying the strategy most likely to succeed and are a popular tool in machine learning.

Application of AI

Artificial Intelligence has numerous applications in today's society. Nowadays, it has become crucial because it can solve complex problems in many industries, such as medical, entertainment, finance, and education, and can make your daily life more comfortable and faster. AI can be used in various forms across multiple fields and continues to expand rapidly.

1. Healthcare

In the last ten years, AI has been increasingly used in the healthcare industry. It has proved to be a game-changer, improving every part of the industry virtually. In the future, it is expected to have a significant impact on this industry.

Healthcare organizations/institutions are using AI for better and faster diagnosis. AI can help doctors make a diagnosis and can tell patients when their condition will be deteriorated so that they can provide medical assistance to patients before being hospitalized.

AI-enabled workflow assistants are aiding doctors to free-up their schedules. These assistants reduce time and cost by streamlining processes and opening up new avenues for the industry. Also, AI-powered technology helps pathologists analyze tissue samples and make a more accurate diagnosis.

A clinical decision support system developed by Cambio Health Care helps in stroke prevention. It can give physicians a warning when the patient is at risk of having a stroke.

Coala, a real-time heart monitoring system, introduced a digitalized device that can find cardiac diseases.

AI in healthcare doesn't need us to develop a new medication. Just by using an existing drug in the right way, you can save lives.

2. Marketing

Marketing is a method of sugar-coating products to fascinate more customers. Humans are good at sugar coating, but what if you only build algorithms or robots to market brands or companies? In the early 2000s, if you would search online stores to find products without knowing its exact name, it might have become a nightmare. But now, when you search for products in any e-commerce store, you get all possible results related to the topic. Like these search engines are reading your minds. After a few seconds, you will get a list of all related items. For example, 'find the right movie on Netflix'.

As discussed in the previous chapter, one of the reasons users are addicted to Netflix is its highly accurate prediction technology, which uses "customer response to movies." To recommend shows and movies, it checks millions of records. You may like it based on previous actions and movie choices. This technology becomes smarter every day with the growing data set. Soon AI will enable online consumers to buy products by clicking photos.

3. Banking

AI-based systems are helping banks deliver customer support, detect anomalies, and prevent credit card frauds. An Electronic Virtual Assistant (EVA) is assisting a leading bank by processing customer queries. To date, EVA has processed more than 3,000,000 customer queries, interacted with more than 500,000 unique users, and conducted more than 1,000,000 conversations. EVA can gather information from thousands of sources and provide answers in less than 0.4 seconds.

Using AI for fraud prevention is not new. AI solutions can be used to upgrade the security of many business sectors, including retail and finance. By tracking card usage and endpoint access, security experts can prevent fraud more effectively. Organizations use AI to monitor and analyze trading behavior. Companies like MasterCard and RBS WorldPay have been using AI and deep learning technologies, and it saved millions of dollars for them.

4. Gaming

Most video games -including "racing" games, shooting games, or strategy games – have different components supported by AI or related applications. Enemy robots and neutral characters are common examples. The primary purpose of using AI in games is to provide players with realistic gaming experience, enabling them to contend with each other on a virtual platform. Also, the AI in the game can improve players' interest and satisfaction in the long run. AI is being used extensively in the gaming industry.

These days, games are not just for entertainment and passing the time, but it can design intelligent agents that can compete with humans. AlphaGo is a computer program that can play the strategy game "Go."

Today, the gaming industry is among the most profitable sectors, and according to experts by 2022, the revenue of the gaming industry will be USD 196 million. As it continues to grow, the demands of the gaming community and the game itself are also evolving. The need for realism in games is higher than ever. Artificial intelligence plays a vital role in making games more interactive, immersive, and intelligent. With the rapid development of new AI technologies and algorithms, this is an exciting time for game developers to show their full potential.

5. Finance

The financial sector relies heavily on real-time reporting, accuracy, and processing of large amounts of quantitative data to make key decisions. AI-enabled systems outperform all these aspects. Because of the accuracy and efficiency of AI, the financial sector is rapidly implementing ML, adaptive intelligence, algorithmic trading, chatbots, automation, etc.

into many processes, e.g., identify fraud, detect anti-money laundering pattern and many more.

Automated advisors, powered by AI, can predict the best portfolio or stock based on preferences by scanning the market data. AI can also generate actionable reports based on relevant financial data by scanning millions of crucial data points and saving analysts numerous hours of work.

6. Data Security/Cyber Security:

Emerging technologies put cybersecurity at risk. Even new developments in security, professionals' defense strategies sometimes fail. Also, with the continuous development of offense and defense strategies and innovation, the complexity and number of cyber-attacks are increasing. Security experts combine the advantages of artificial intelligence (AI) with network security and have additional resources to defend against vulnerable networks and data from cyber attackers. Compared with what traditional security methods usually anticipate or require, artificial intelligence security involves using artificial intelligence to identify and stop cyber threats with less manual intervention.

AI can save time and money by quickly browsing structured data and thoroughly reading and learning unstructured data, statistical information, words, and phrases. It can be used to provide proactive and quick responses to new challenges, which may be before humans discover new challenges. Artificial Intelligence-driven security tools can reduce risks and even manage many threats to data security. They can do this through automation and inspection of themselves, or by providing enhanced functionality for the security team and security operations center (SOC). It helps reduce SQL injection, denial of service (DOS) attacks, data leakage, ransomware, etc.

AEG bot and AI2 Platforms are used to detect software bugs and cyber-attacks.

---

7. Security and surveillance

Imagine a single person monitoring multiple video cameras—indeed, a stressful and tedious job to do. But AI can help to automate it.

The video surveillance system powered by AI can detect crimes before they happen. They track unusual behavior of people (standing motionless for a long time, stumbling, or napping on benches, etc.).

The system can warn its human attendants that they can take action to avoid accidents. Moreover, when such activities are reported and counted as accurate, they will further help improve monitoring services through back-end machine learning. Technologies such as facial recognition and speech recognition are getting better with each passing day. Image processing technology uses data science to assist artificial intelligence.

Surveillance, a targeted form of monitoring, is usually carried out to obtain specific data or evidence, and often occurs when people do not know that they are being monitored, such as collecting data from applications without knowing it. The US, China, and Germany have the best surveillance cameras in the world. China is the undisputed leader, and the number of surveillance cameras installed in its territory is four times that of the United States.

8. Smart home devices

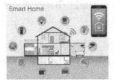

Artificial intelligence can make a "smart home" a reality. Most smart home devices you buy use AI to learn your behavior, so they can automatically adjust settings to make your experience as frictionless as possible. Smart voice assistants control these smart home devices, again an AI. Some of the best Smart Home Devices are Echo Plus – Best Smart Speaker, Nest Learning Thermostat – Best Energy-

---

Saving Smart Thermostat, Amazon Echo Dot – Best Smart Home Hub, and many more.

Smart lights can change intensity and color based on time, and thermostats can adjust the temperature based on user preference.

9. Social Media

Facebook, Twitter, and Snapchat contain billions of user profiles, which need to be stored and managed in a super-efficient manner. AI can organize and manage a large amount of data and can analyze it to identify the latest trends, hashtags, and requirements of different users. From the notifications received to the feeds seen in the timeline, all content is managed by AI. AI will understand your past web searches, interactions, behaviors, and all other things you have done while visiting these websites, and tailor your experience based on these observations.

The role and complexity of artificial intelligence grow with increasing content in the platforms. Because then, it has to fight spam and improve user experience.

10. Travel & Transport

AI can make end-to-end travel arrangements: suggesting hotels, flights, and best routes to the customers. Travel industries are using AI-powered chatbots for better and faster response to customers. In both the travel and transportation industries, AI is steadily becoming one of the vital service tools for both service providers and users. Travel companies are capitalizing on the ubiquitous usage of smart devices. Most users, with the help of AI-powered travel assistants, view trips, research landmarks, and dining options locally, and book trips on these devices. Chatbots assist in travel recommendations, better booking prices, and faster response times. Google Maps scan road information and utilizes algorithms to identify the optimal route to take, by bike, car, bus, train, or on foot.

---

11. Autonomous vehicles and drones

For the last few decades, self-driving cars have been the buzzword in the AI industry. The development of autonomous vehicles is revolutionizing the transportation system. Waymo conducted several test drives at Phoenix before deploying its first AI-based public ride service. The AI system collects data from the "vehicle's radar," cloud services, cameras, and GPS to build control signals that operate the vehicle. Advanced deep learning algorithms can accurately predict things than come "near the vehicle." Therefore, Waymo's cars are more efficient and safer. A large segment of autonomous vehicles is connected and, thus, can share the information.

In Tesla's self-driving car AI implements computer vision, image detection, and deep learning to operate cars that can automatically detect objects and drive without human intervention. Large companies like Wal-Mart and Amazon have already invested heavily in drone delivery plans. Expect more investments in the future. With self-driving vehicles traveling on the road and self-driving drones delivering goods, many transportations and service-related challenges can be resolved faster and more effectively.

12. Robotics

Usually, robots are programmed to perform some repetitive tasks. Still, with the help of AI, you can create intelligent robots that can perform tasks with their own experiences without being pre-programmed. Robots have sensors and actuators that can-do different things. These sensors can see things in front of them and measure the temperature, heat, movements, and so on. They have processors on board that compute various information in real-time. They are also capable of adapting to new environments. *Humanoid robots Erica and Sophia can talk and behave like humans.*

---

13. Media & Entertainment industry

The way content is distributed is changing the world over, and the global media and entertainment industry is a witness to this rapid transformation. With the help of ubiquitous content creation tools like high-resolution cameras, smartphones, and content creation software, pretty much anyone can create, publish, and distribute different forms of content (write-ups, audios, and videos).

AI is helping the companies in the media and entertainment industry improve their services and upgrade their customer experience. Here are a few AI use cases:

13.1. Metadata tagging:

AI-based video intelligence tools can analyze the contents of a video frame by frame and attach appropriate tags to them. Prominent media creators and distributors like CBS interactive are using this. This can be a painful manual task to perform.

13.2. Content personalization:

Popular music and video streaming platforms like Spotify and Netflix are using AI and ML algorithms to study user behavior and demographics. The algorithms recommend what their consumers may be most interested in listening to or watching next and help in keeping them engaged. These AI-based platforms are providing customers the content that caters to their unique likings, thus offering them a highly personalized experience.

13.3. Reporting automation:

Aside from automating day-to-day or minute-by-minute operations, AI is helping media companies in strategic decision-making. Big media and broadcasting companies are using natural language generation and ML and to create channel performance reports from raw data.

AI-enabled data analysis and natural language generation-based reporting automation tools, help business leaders create performance reports. These algorithms have easy-to-understand language commentaries, and they arrive at accurate insights that help in making informed data-driven decisions.

13.4. Subtitle generation:

International media publishing companies need their content fit for consumption by multi-region audiences. To do so, they need to provide accurate multilingual subtitles for their video content. Human translators can take hundreds or thousands of years to write subtitles for various movies and shows manually.

14. Agriculture

Artificial Intelligence in agriculture is helping farmers increase efficiency and productivity and reduce the negative impact on the environment. Artificial Intelligence technology can help the agricultural sector produce healthier crops, control pests, and monitor the soil. Under growing conditions, it can organize data for farmers, provide workload assistance, and advance a wide range of agriculture-related tasks throughout the food supply chain. These innovations in agriculture are driven by climate change, population growth, and food security issues. Therefore, the use of AI in agriculture can make farmers around the world more efficient, enabling farms of all sizes to operate and maintain the world's food supply.

Using artificial intelligence in agriculture can help farmers understand data insights such as temperature, precipitation, wind speed, and solar radiation. Data analysis of historical value can better understand the required results. The best part of implementing AI in agriculture is that it "will not eliminate the work of human farmers." On the contrary, it will improve their processes. Artificial Intelligence provides a more effective way to produce, harvest, and sell essential crops in the following ways:

- Checking defective crops and improving healthy crop production.
- Strengthening agro-based businesses to run more efficiently.
- Automating machine adjustments for weather forecasting and disease or pest identification.
- Improving crop management practices, thus, helping many tech businesses invest in algorithms useful in agriculture.
- AI-driven technologies assist farmers in optimizing planning and create more generous yields by determining crop choices, the best hybrid seed, and resource utilization.
- Helping farmers address climate variation, pests, and weeds infestation.

AI can identify a disease with 98% accuracy. Farmers can use AI to manage weeds by implementing computer vision, robotics, and machine learning. With the help of the AI, data are gathered to keep a check on weeds, which helps the farmers spray chemicals only where the weeds are present— thus limiting the amount of chemical spray Identifying or monitoring defects and nutrient deficiencies in the soil. With image recognition, AI identifies possible defects through captured images, helping farmers remain updated with weather forecasting. The forecasted/predicted data help farmers increase yields and profits without risking the crop.

15. Personalized shopping experience (E-commerce)
AI is helping shoppers to find related products with recommended sizes, colors, and even brands. To this end, the online shopping platform you use collects and stores much information about your usage, whether you like it or not.

With AI, online stores can use the smallest piece of data about every link you follow or hover to and use it to personalize your experience on a deeper level. This information is used to give you timely alerts, messages, visuals that may interest you, and dynamic content that modifies according to demand and supply.

Online stores can also automatically change currency and interface, send notifications about discounts on best-selling products, and offer time limits on desirable items.

Google Analytics can provide online store information like your location, your browser, device, etc., along with the time you spend on each page.

16. Education:

The education world is becoming more convenient and personalized because of the numerous AI applications. They have changed the way people learn because educational materials are becoming accessible to all with the help of smart devices and computers. Now, students don't need to attend physical classes to study if they have a personal computer and an internet connection. AI is also automating administrative tasks, allowing educators to spend more time with students.

AI in education usually focuses on identifying what a student does and 'doesn't know. It does so with the help of diagnostic testing and by developing personalized curricula for each student's specific needs. Derek Li, the founder of Chinese EdTech unicorn Squirrel AI, says: "In three hours you understand students more than the three years spent by the best teachers."

These are the benefits brought by AI in education:

16.1. Automating Administrative Tasks: AI can automate the administrative tasks of educators and academic institutions. At present, teachers spend a lot of time on grading exams, responding to students, and assessing homework. AI can grade multiple tests.

16.2. Smart Content: Smart content includes virtual content like video lectures and video conferencing. AI systems use traditional syllabuses to create customized books for specific subjects. With AI, textbooks are getting digitized, and new learning interfaces are being designed to help students across academic grades and ages.

16.3. Personalized Learning: AI may not necessarily replace teachers, but they can perform better by offering personalized recommendations. AI customizes in-class assignments and final exams, ensuring the best possible assistance to students.

16.4. Global Learning: AI can help eliminate boundaries. It can facilitate the learning of any course from anywhere across the globe and at any time.

16.5. New Efficiencies: AI improves IT processes and brings out new efficiencies. Schools can use it to prevent students from getting lost in crowds when they run in corridors. AI can also be used to model complex data enabling the operations to create data-driven forecasts.

17. Automated customer support

Today, 'you'd hardly find a good online store that 'doesn't offer at least one form of high-tech customer support in addition to the traditional support channel that can be reached via email or phone. Traditional support channels cost companies a huge amount of waste of capital and human resources, which could have been used directly for more intelligent and creative tasks. AI-enabled customer assistants can answer simple questions, such as letting you know the status of your order and help you find specific products based on descriptions.

Chatbots can enhance the shopping experience in the following ways:

- Increasing user retention by sending reminders and notifications.
- Offering instant answers, thus reducing response time.
- Providing upselling opportunities through a personalized approach.

18. Chatbots

Almost every modern household today has a virtual assistant to control the appliances at home. Siri and Cortana are gaining popularity because of the user experience they provide. Amazon's Echo uses speech recognition and NLP to perform a wide range of tasks on your command. Other than playing your favorite songs, it can be used to control home devices, book cabs, make phone calls, order food, check the weather conditions, and so on. 'Google's virtual assistant, Google Duplex, can not only respond to calls and book appointments for you, but it can also add a human touch.

With the help of Natural Language Processing (NLP) and machine learning, the device can process human language and perform tasks such as managing schedules, making a reservation, controlling a smart home, and so on.

19. Creative arts

Artificial intelligence technology is inspiring new songs. Based on information gathered from millions of newspaper headlines, conversations, and speeches, insights can be collected that can help musicians create topics. Watson BEAT can help composers by proposing different musical elements. By harnessing the power of artificial intelligence, musicians can

---

understand the needs of listeners and create songs based on these insights. IBM's AI-powered Chef Watson is part of IBM's mission to develop cognitive computing applications that can improve medical research by creating amazing new formulations to help people discover new ideas.

MuseNet can now write classical music to echo the classical legends, Bach and Mozart. It is a deep neural network that can generate 4 minutes of musical composition with ten different instruments and can combine the musical styles of the country, Mozart, and Beetle. MuseNet discovers patterns of harmony, style, and rhythm through self-learning. "Wordsmith" is a natural language generation platform that can transform data into insightful narratives.

Machine Learning Algorithms

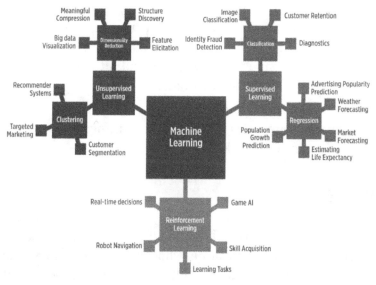

No Free Lunch

In ML, there's the "No Free Lunch" theorem. In short, it points out that no algorithm can solve every problem well, and it is particularly relevant to supervised learning (i.e., predictive modeling). For example, you cannot say that neural networks are always better than decision trees and vice versa.

There are many factors to ponder, such as the size and structure of the data set. Therefore, you should try many different algorithms for your problem, and then choose the algorithm that works best.

Machine learning can be grouped into three broad learning tasks: Supervised, Unsupervised, and Reinforcement Learning.

Supervised Learning

An algorithm uses training data and human feedback to learn the relationship between a given input and output. In "supervised learning," you will use well-labeled data to train the machine. This means that some information has been marked as the correct answer. The supervised learning algorithm learns from the labeled training data and predicts outcomes for new data.

For instance, a practitioner can use marketing expenses and weather forecasts as input data to predict the sales of cans. Supervised learning is used when the output data is known. The algorithm will predict new data.

Types of Supervised Learning

There are two categories of supervised learning:

- ❖ Classification task
- ❖ Regression task

Classification

Classification is to group the output into a class. If the algorithm attempts to label the input as two different classes, it is called binary classification. Choosing between more than two categories is called multi-class classification. For example, predict employee turnover, email spam, financial fraud, or student letter grades.

Suppose you want to predict the gender of an advertiser. You will start to collect data about height, weight, work, salary, shopping basket, etc. from the customer database. You know the gender of each customer, which can be male, female, or X. The goal of the classifier is based on the information (i.e., the features you collect).

The goal of the classifier will be to assign a probability of being any of the above three (i.e., the label) based on the information (i.e., features you have collected).

When the model learns how to recognize gender, you can use new data to make a prediction. For instance, you just got further information from an unknown customer, and you want to know if it is a male, female or X. If the classifier predicts 70% male, it means that the algorithm can determine that 70% of the customers are male and 30% are female or X.

Regression

A task is considered as a regression task when the output is a continuous value. Regression techniques use training data to predict a single output value. For example, a financial analyst may need to predict the value of a stock based on a series of characteristics (such as stocks, previous stock performance, macroeconomic indicators, etc.). To estimate the stock price with the smallest possible error, the system will be trained. You can use regression to predict house prices from training data. The input variables will be location, house size, etc.

Types of Regression methods

Logistic Regression

Logistic regression is the categorical counterpart of linear regression. The prediction is mapped between 0 and 1 by a logical function, which means that the prediction can be interpreted as a class probability. The models themselves are still "linear," so when your classes are linearly separable (i.e., they can be separated by a single decision surface), they work well.

Strengths:
- The algorithm can be regularized to avoid overfitting, and outputs can have an excellent probabilistic interpretation.
- With new data and by using stochastic gradient descent, logistic models can be easily updated.

Weaknesses:
- Logistic regression has shown a tendency to underperform when limited by multiple or non-linear decision boundaries.
- They are inflexible and cannot capture complex relationships.

Naïve Bayes (NB) Classifiers

Naïve Bayesian model is easy to build and very useful for large datasets. It is a straightforward algorithm based on conditional probability. This method consists of a direct acyclic graph with a parent and several child nodes. It assumes independence between child nodes separated from the parent node. Naive Bayes algorithm is mainly used for sentiment analysis, spam filtering, recommendation system, and many more. They are quick and simple to implement; however, their biggest disadvantage is that the predictors must be independent.

Strength:

Although the conditional independence assumption is rarely established, the NB model performs surprisingly well in practice.
- They can be quickly implemented and scaled up.

Weakness:
- Because of their simplicity, NB models are often surpassed by models sufficiently tuned and trained by the above-listed algorithms.

Decision Trees

Decisions trees classify occurrence by sorting them based on the feature value. In this, each node is the feature of an example. The node must be classified, and every branch must represent a value that the node can take. It is an extensively used technique for classification. In this method, the classification is a tree called a decision tree.

Strengths:

- The decision tree forces the consideration of all possible outcomes of a decision and traces each path to a conclusion.
- It creates a comprehensive analysis of the consequences along each branch and identifies decision nodes that need further investigation.

Weaknesses:

- Every time a new training set gets added, it needs to be remodeled.
- Likely to get overfitted, especially with data with high variance (a lot of features). One way to stop is to limit the growth of the tree before it reaches one data point.
- It fits the noise.

Decision Tree for Play Tennis

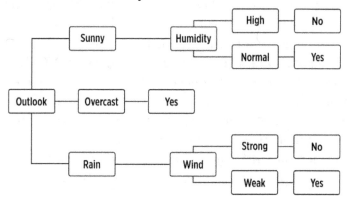

Support Vector Machine (SVM)

SVM is a supervised machine learning algorithm that can be used for classification or regression problems. It uses a technique called kernel tricks to transform your data, and then based on these transformations, finds an optimal boundary that maximizes the distance between the closest members of each class. It performs some extremely complex data transformations, and then figure out how to separate the data based on the tags or outputs you define.

Strength:
These can model non-linear decision boundaries and have an array of kernels to choose from. They are also considerably immune against overfitting, especially in high-dimensional space.

Weakness:
They are memory intensive, difficult to scale up and, trickier to tune because of the value of picking the right kernel. At present, random forests are usually preferred over SVM's.

K- Nearest Neighbors (KNN):

The K-Nearest Neighbor (KNN) algorithm is a simple, easy-to-implement, supervised machine learning algorithm that can be used to solve classification and regression problems. In pattern recognition, the k-nearest neighbor algorithm (k-NN) is a non-parametric method used for classification and regression. In the above case, the input consists of the k closest training examples in the feature space. The output depends on which task (classification or regression) KNN is used for: In classification, the output is a class member. Inputs are classified by plurality votes from their neighbors, and the input is assigned to the commonest category of its k nearest neighbors (k is a positive integer, usually small).
If k = 1, then only the object is assigned to the class of this single nearest neighbor. In regression, the output is the

---

attribute value of the object. This value is calculated as the average of the values of the k-nearest neighbors.

A lazy learning algorithm is simply an algorithm where the algorithm generalizes the data after a query is made. The best example of this is the KNN. K-Nearest Neighbor stores all the points then use that data when you make a query to it. K-NN is a lazy learner because it doesn't learn a discriminative function from the training data but "memorizes" the training dataset instead.

Where is KNN used?

KNN is a non-parametric lazy learning algorithm. The purpose is to use a database that divides data points into several categories to predict the classification of new sampling points. For reference only, this is the "position" of KNN in the list of algorithms learned by sci-kit.

Strengths:

- Fit for noisy training data.
- It can detect non-linear or linear distributed data.
- It takes no assumptions about the underlying data or its distribution and therefore is non-parametric.

Weaknesses:

- Its non-parametric feature makes it slow in querying (vs. fast in training).
- It can be sensitive to outliers.

AdaBoost

AdaBoost(Adaptive Boosting) is an ML meta-algorithm that combines a number of "weak classifiers" into a single "strong classifier." Here are some facts about AdaBoost:

- In AdaBoost, the weak learners are decision trees with a single split, and they are called decision stumps.
- AdaBoost works by putting more weight on difficult to classify instances and less on those already handled well.

- AdaBoost algorithms can be used for both classification and regression problems.

Strengths:
- It is fast, simple, and easy to program.
- It has the flexibility to be combined with any machine learning algorithm.

Weaknesses:
- It is from empirical evidence and particularly vulnerable to uniform noise.
- Weak classifiers, being too weak can lead to low margins and overfitting.

Random Forest

Random Forest is a supervised learning algorithm, used for classification and regression because you know that the forest is composed of trees, and more trees mean a stronger forest. Similarly, the random forest algorithm creates a decision tree on data samples, then obtains predictions from each sample, and finally uses voting to select the best solution. It is an ensemble method, better than a single decision tree, as it reduces overfitting by averaging the results.

Strengths:
- It handles high-dimensional spaces very well.
- It lessens high variance.
- It does not expect features that are linear in nature or interact linearly.
- It improves the robustness of the classifier when used on decision trees.

Weakness:
   A combination of decision trees is harder to interpret than a single tree.

Gradient boosting model (GBM)

Gradient boosting is a machine learning technique used for regression and classification problems. It generates

---

prediction models in the form of a set of weak prediction models (usually decision trees). It relies on the intuition that when the best next model is used in combination with the previous model, the overall prediction error can be minimized. The vital idea is to set the target outcomes for the next model to reduce the mistakes.

Strengths:

- It provides predictive accuracy that cannot be beaten.
- Since boosted trees are derived by optimizing an objective function, GBM can be used to solve almost all objective functions that you can write gradient out.
- Lots of flexibility – It can optimize different loss functions and provides several hyperparameter tuning options that make the function fit very flexible.
- No data pre-processing required – works excellent with categorical and numerical values as is.
- Handles missing data – imputation is not required.

Weaknesses:

- Training takes longer because trees are built sequentially.
- GBMs are more sensitive to overfitting if the data is noisy.
- GBMs are harder to tune than Random Forest.
- GBMs are computationally expensive and require many trees (>1000), which can consume both time and memory.

Challenges in Supervised Machine Learning

- Irrelevant input training data could give inaccurate results
- Data preparation and pre-processing are a challenge.
- Brute force is needed if the concerned expert is not available. The user needs to think about the right features (input variables) to train the machine on. This can be inaccurate.

Advantages of Supervised Learning:

- Allows data collection or data output production from previous experience
- Helps in optimizing performance criteria using experience
- Helps in solving various types of real-world computation problems.

Disadvantages of Supervised Learning

- In the absence of desired examples in the training set, the decision boundary might be over-trained
- While training the classifier, many good examples from each class are needed.
- Classifying big data can be a challenge.
- Time consuming.

Unsupervised learning

Unsupervised learning is an ML technique, in which a supervised model isn't needed. Instead, the model needs to be allowed to work on its own to find information. It mainly deals with unlabeled data. Unsupervised learning algorithms will enable you to perform complex processing tasks, but this is unpredictable. In unsupervised learning, the algorithm explores input data without knowing the explicit output variables (for example, exploring customer demographic data to identify patterns). You can use it when you don't know how to classify the data and want the algorithm to find patterns for you and classify the data.

Why Unsupervised Learning?

- Finds all kinds of unknown patterns in data.
- Helps you find useful features for categorization.
- Happens in real-time, so all the input data to be analyzed and labeled takes place in the presence of learners.

- Gets data quickly because it is easier to get unlabeled data from a computer than labeled data, which needs manual intervention.

Types of Unsupervised Learning

Unsupervised learning problems are of two kinds:
- Clustering
- Association

Clustering

The clustering process looks for structures or patterns in a collection of unclassified data. The clustering algorithm will process your data and find natural clusters (groups) (if they exist in the data). You can also modify the number of clusters that the algorithm should recognize. You can adjust the granularity of groups with this.

Clustering Types
- Hierarchical clustering
- K-means clustering
- K-NN (k nearest neighbors)
- Principal Component Analysis
- Singular Value Decomposition
- Independent Component Analysis

Hierarchical Clustering:

Hierarchical clustering analysis or HCA is an unsupervised clustering algorithm that involves creating clusters with a predominant order from top to bottom. For example, all files and folders on the hard disk are organized in a hierarchical structure. The algorithm divides similar objects into groups called clusters.

Treat two close clusters as the same cluster. When there is only one cluster left, the algorithm ends. This clustering technique is divided into two types:
- Aggregate hierarchical clustering
- Divided hierarchical clustering

K-means Clustering

K-means clustering is unsupervised learning, used when you have unlabeled data (that is, data with no defined categories or groups). K-means is one of the simplest algorithms to solve a well-known clustering problem. The objective of the algorithm is to find groups in the data, the number of groups is characterized by the variable K. The algorithm iteratively assigns each data point to one of the K groups according to the provided functions. Clusters have data points based on feature similarity. The result of the K-means clustering algorithm is:
1. The centroids of K clusters can be used to mark new data
2. The label of the training data (each data point is assigned to a cluster)
With clustering, you do not need to define groups before looking for data, but you can find and analyze organically formed groups. The "Select K" section below describes how to determine the number of groups. Each centroid of the cluster is a collection of element values that define the resulting group. Checking the centroid feature weights can be used to explain the qualitative representation of each cluster.

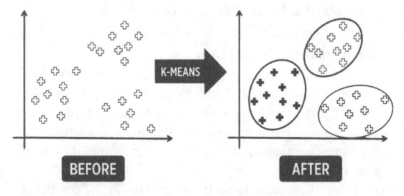

Principal Components Analysis (PCA):

PCA is a dimensionality reduction method that is commonly used to reduce the dimensionality of large data sets by converting large variable sets into smaller variable sets (which still contain most of the information in the large set).

Reducing the number of data set variables will naturally come at the cost of accuracy. Nonetheless, the trick to dimensionality reduction sacrifices some accuracy at the expense of simplicity, because smaller data sets are easier to browse and visualize, and make data analysis easier and more quickly perform machine learning algorithms without having to deal with other variables. So, in summary, the idea of PCA is simple – reduce the number of variables in the data set while retaining the possible information.

Association

Association rules allow you to establish associations between data objects within large databases. Association discovers new relationships between variables in large databases. For example, people who buy a new home are likely to buy new furniture.

Other Examples:

- A subgroup of cancer patients based on their gene measurements
- Groups of shoppers based on their browsing and purchasing histories
- A movie group based on the rating given by movie viewers

Applications of Unsupervised Machine Learning

Some applications of unsupervised machine learning techniques are:

- Clustering: Based on the similarity of the data set, automatically divide it into several groups
- Anomaly detection: discover unusual data points in your dataset. It is useful for finding fraudulent transactions
- Association mining: identify sets of items which often occur together in your dataset

---

- Latent variable models: use for data pre-processing. Like cutting the number of features in a dataset or splitting the dataset into multiple components

Disadvantages of Unsupervised Learning

- You cannot get accurate information about data sorting, and the data output used in unsupervised learning is labeled and unknown
- The accuracy of the results is low because the input data is unknown, and no one has labeled it in advance. This means that the machine does it.
- Spectral classes do not always correspond to information classes.
- Users need to spend time explaining and labeling the class.
- The spectral properties of a class may also change with time, so when moving from one image to another, you will not be able to obtain the same class information.

Supervised vs. Unsupervised Learning

Parameter	Supervised machine learning technique	Unsupervised machine learning technique
Process	Input and output variables will be given.	Only input data will be given
Input Data	Algorithms are trained using labeled data.	Algorithms are used against un-labeled data
Algorithms Used	Support vector machine, Linear and logistics regression, Neural network, Random forest, and Classification trees.	Cluster algorithms, K-means, Hierarchical clustering, etc.
Computational complexity	A simpler method.	Computationally complex
Use of Data	Uses training data to learn the link between the input and the output.	Does not use output data.
Accuracy of results	Highly accurate and trustworthy method.	Less accurate and trustworthy method.
Real-Time Learning	Offline.	Real-time.
Number of Classes	Known.	Unknown.
Limitations	Classifying big data can be problematic	Precise information regarding data sorting is not available, and as data used is Un-labeled, the output is not known.

Deep Learning

Deep learning computer software imitates the network of neurons in a brain. A neural network is an architecture of layers stacked on top of each other. It is a subset of ML and is called deep learning because it uses deep neural networks. In deep learning, the machine uses different layers to learn from the given data. The number of layers in the model represents its depth.

Deep learning algorithms are constructed with connected layers.

- Input Layer is the first layer
- Output Layer is the last layer
- All layers in between are called Hidden Layers. The word 'deep' means the network joins neurons in more than two layers.

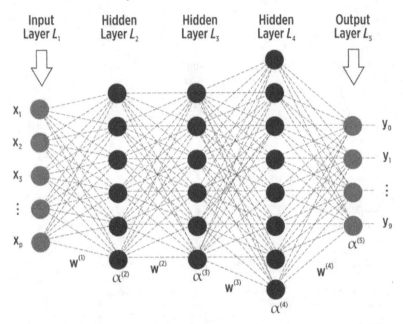

Each hidden layer consists of neurons that are connected. The neuron will process it and then propagate the input signal received from the layer above it. The strength of the signal passed to the next layer of neurons depends on weight, bias, and activation function.

The network consumes a lot of input data and operates through multiple layers. The network can learn increasingly complex data features at each layer. Deep neural networks can provide state-of-the-art accuracy in many tasks, from object detection to speech recognition. It can learn automatically without the programmer's pre-defined knowledge that is explicitly coded.

Each layer signifies a deeper level of knowledge. Compared with a two-layer neural network, a four-layer neural network will learn more complex features. Learning is divided into two stages.

- The first stage involves nonlinearly transforming the input and creating a Statistical model as output.
- The second phase aims at the derivative (mathematical method, which aims at improving the model).

The neural network repeats these two stages hundreds to thousands of times until it reaches a tolerable level of accuracy. Repeating these two stages is called iteration.

Why is Deep Learning Important?

Deep learning is a powerful tool to convert prediction into actionable results. It is good at pattern discovery (unsupervised learning) and knowledge-based prediction. Big data is the driving force of deep learning. When the two are combined, organizations can achieve unprecedented results in productivity, sales, management, and innovation. Deep learning can outperform traditional methods. Its algorithms are more accurate than machine learning algorithms; 41% more in image classification; 27 % more in facial recognition and 25% more in voice recognition.

Limitations of Deep Learning

Data labeling

Almost all recent AI models are trained through "supervised learning." This means that humans must label and classify the basic data, which can be quite large and error-prone. Companies that develop self-driving car technology are hiring hundreds of people to manually annotate hours of video in prototype vehicles to help train these systems.

Get a huge training dataset

It has been shown that in some of the cases, simple deep learning techniques like CNN can imitate expert knowledge in medicine and other fields. However, the current wave of machine learning requires training data sets to be not only labeled but also sufficiently broad and general.

Deep learning methods require thousands of observations to make the model relatively good at the classification of tasks, and in some cases, millions of observations to perform at the human level. Not surprisingly, deep learning is prevalent among large technology companies. They are using big data to accumulate PB data. It enables them to create impressive and highly accurate deep learning models.

The Interpretation Problem

Large and complex models may be difficult to interpret from a human perspective. It is one of the reasons for the slow acceptance of certain AI tools in the application field. In areas where interpretability is useful or indeed requires interpretability, AI may be slow to merge. As AI applications expand, regulatory requirements may also require more interpretable AI models.

Machine Learning vs. Deep Learning

In the table below, the difference between machine learning and deep learning has been summarized.

	Machine Learning	Deep Learning
Data Requirements	Fit for small/medium dataset	Fit for large dataset
Hardware Requirements	Works on a low-end machine	Requires powerful machine, preferably with GPU
Feature engineering	Need to understand the features that represent the data	No need to understand the best feature that represents the data
Interpretability	Interpretation of algorithms vary: Some are easy (logistic, decision tree), some are difficult (SVM, XGBoost)	Difficult to impossible
Number of algorithms	Many	Few
Training time	Short	Long (days to a week)
Accuracy	Less accurate	More accurate than machine learning

Neural Networks

Neural networks are a series of algorithms designed to identify potential relationships in a set of data by mimicking the way the human brain operates. Meaning neural networks are a collection of layers of computational units called neurons, connected in different layers. These networks convert the data until it can be classified as output. Each neuron multiplies the initial value by a certain weight, adds the result to other values entering the same neuron, adjusts the number of results by the deviation of the neuron, and then uses the activation function to normalize the output.

Classification of Neural Networks

Shallow neural network: Shallow neural network has only one hidden layer between input and output.

Deep neural network: Deep neural network has multiple layers. For example, the Google LeNet model for image recognition has 22 layers.

Nowadays, deep learning is used in a driverless car, mobile phones, Google search engine, fraud detection, TV, and many other applications.

Feed-forward neural networks: This is the simplest type of artificial neural network. In these networks, the information flows in only one direction, forward. It means, the information flow starts at the input layer, goes to the "hidden" layers, and ends at the output layer. The network does not have a loop.

Recurrent neural networks (RNNs): RNN is a multi-layer neural network that can store information in context nodes, thus enabling it to learn data sequences and output numbers or other sequences. In simple words, it is an artificial neural network connecting neurons in loops. RNNs are well-suited for processing sequences of inputs.

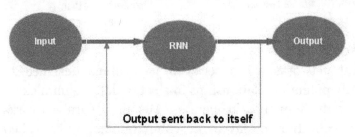

For example, RNN can be used to predict the next word in a sentence: "Do you want to...?"

- The RNN neuron will receive a signal pointing to the beginning of the sentence.

- The network gets the word "Do" as an input and produces a vector of the number. This vector is inputted to the neuron to give a memory to the network. This stage helps the network remember the "Do" it received, and it received it in the first place.
- The network will similarly enter the next word. It uses the terms "you" and "want." After receiving each word, the state of the neuron is updated.
- The concluding stage occurs after receiving the word "a." The neural network will provide each English word with a probability that it can be used to complete a sentence. A well-trained RNN may assign higher opportunities to "cafe," "drink," "hamburger," etc.

Common uses of RNN

- Help securities traders to generate analytic reports
- Detect abnormalities in financial statement contracts
- Detect fraudulent credit-card transaction
- Provide a caption for images
- Power chatbots
- Commonly used when the practitioners are working with time-series data or sequences (e.g., audio recordings or text).

Convolutional neural networks (CNN)

CNN is a multi-layer neural network with a unique architecture designed to extract increasingly complex features from each layer of data to determine the output. CNN is very suitable for perception tasks. CNN is usually used when there are unstructured data sets (such as images), and practitioners need to extract information from it. For example, if the goal is to predict the image caption:

- Let's assume that CNN receives an image of a cat. In computer terms, this image is a collection of pixels-usually, one layer is used for grayscale pictures, and three layers are used for color pictures.

- During feature learning (i.e., hidden layer), the network will recognize unique features, for example, the cat's tail, ears, etc.
- When the network has thoroughly learned how to recognize pictures, it can provide probabilities for each image it knows. The label with the highest probability is the prediction of the network.

Reinforcement Learning (RL)

- Reinforcement learning (RL) is an ML technique that enables agents to use feedback on their behavior and experience to learn in an interactive environment through trial and error. In this system, by receiving virtual "rewards" or "punishments" for training, Google's DeepMind defeated human champions in Go games through reinforcement learning. Reinforcement learning improves the gaming experience in video games by providing smarter robots.
- Although both supervised learning and reinforcement learning use the mapping between input and output, unlike supervised learning, in supervised learning, the feedback provided to the agent is the correct set of actions to perform the task, while reinforcement learning treats rewards and punishments as positive and negative behavioral signals.
- Compared with unsupervised learning, reinforcement learning has different goals. Although the goal of unsupervised learning is to find similarities and differences between data points, the purpose of reinforcement learning is to find a suitable behavior model that will maximize the agent's total cumulative reward. The following

---

figure shows the basic ideas and elements involved in the reinforcement learning model.

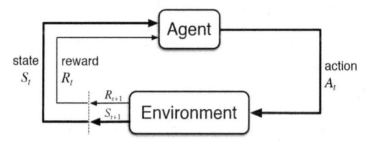

Some of the most famous algorithms are:
- Q-learning
- Deep Q network
- State-Action-Reward-State-Action (SARSA)
- Deep Deterministic Policy Gradient (DDPG)

AI Use cases

Finance: The field of financial technology has begun to use AI to save time, reduce costs, and add value. Deep learning changes the lending industry by using robust credit scores. Credit decision-makers can use AI for powerful credit lending applications to use machine intelligence to consider the characteristics and capabilities of applicants, enabling faster and more accurate risk assessments. "Underwrite" is a fintech company that provides AI solutions for credit companies. "underwrite.ai" uses AI to distinguish which applicant is more likely to repay the loan. Their approach radically outperforms traditional methods.

HR: Under Armour's leadership, a sportswear company, has revolutionized recruitment methods and modernized the job seeker experience, with the help of AI.
It reduced hiring time for its retail stores by 35%. The screening and interviewing process became a challenging task for 30000 resumes, which they received in a month. Slow

---

hiring and on-boarding impacted Under Armour's ability in staffing and operations. *Under Armour* partnered with *HireVue*, an AI provider for HR solutions, for both on-demand and live interviews. The results were impressive; they managed to decrease the time to fill by 35% and hired higher quality staff.

Marketing: Artificial intelligence is a valuable tool to meet the challenges of customer service management and personalization. Improved speech recognition and call routing, AI techniques, in call centers allow a more seamless experience for customers. Deep-learning audio analysis enables systems to assess a customer's tone. If the customer responds poorly to the AI chatbots, the system can reroute the conversation to human operators who take over the issue. Artificial Intelligence is also widely used in other industries.

Chapter 3

Cognitive Artificial Intelligence

****

"Data in one system is helping you optimize the outcome of another system. That's what an AI-first company does, that's what an AI-first software product does."

Satya Nadella, CEO, Microsoft

****

Cognitive Computing

Cognitive computing refers to technologies that perform specific tasks to facilitate human intelligence. These are smart decision support systems (DSS) that you have been working with since the beginning of the internet boom. These systems simply use better data, better algorithms to get a better analysis of a massive amount of information with recent breakthroughs in technology.

Using cognitive computing systems help in making improved human decisions everywhere. The list below denotes some of the many applications of cognitive computing: -

1. Speech recognition
2. Sentiment analysis
3. Face detection
4. Risk assessment
5. Fraud detection

How Cognitive Computing Works?

Cognitive computing systems synthesize data from many information sources while weighing context and conflicting evidence to suggest suitable answers. Cognitive systems use data mining, pattern recognition, and natural language processing (NLP) to understand the way the human brain works.

To solve the problems that are supposed to be done by humans, computers require enormous structured and unstructured data. Gradually, cognitive systems learn to refine the way they identify patterns and process data to anticipate new problems and model possible solutions.

Key Attributes of Cognitive Computing:

Cognitive computing systems have the following key attributes:

- **Adaptive:** This is the foremost step in creating a cognitive system based on machine learning. The solution should copy the capacity of the human mind to take in and adjust from the environmental factors. The frameworks can't be customized for a separate assignment. It should be dynamic in data gathering, understanding goals, and requirements.

- **Interactive:** The cognitive solution must interact with all elements in the system like the brain – processor, devices, cloud services, and user. Cognitive systems should interact bidirectionally. They should understand human input and provide pertinent outcomes using natural language processing and deep learning.

- **Iterative and stateful**: The system should "remember" previous interactions in the process and return information appropriate for the specific application. It should be able to define problems by asking questions or finding other sources. This feature requires careful use of data quality and verification methods to ensure that the system is always provided with sufficient information and that the data sources it operates can provide reliable and up-to-date input.

- **Contextual:** They must understand, locate, and pull contextual elements, including meaning, time, syntax, location, regulations, right domain, user's profile, process, task, and goal. They can use a variety of information sources, including structured and unstructured digital information and sensory input (visual, gesture, auditory, or sensor-provided information). Cognitive computing is a subset of AI, and there are many similarities and differences between the two.

Cognitive Computing vs. AI

The technologies behind Cognitive Computing are just like the technologies in the back of AI. These consist of machine learning, deep learning, NLP, neural networks, etc. But they have differences as well.

Cognitive Computing	Artificial Intelligence
Copies human behavior and reasoning to solve complicated problems.	Augments human reasoning to solve complicated problems. Focuses on delivering accurate results.
Simulates the human thinking process to locate solutions for complex problems.	Finds patterns to know or monitor hidden records and locate solutions.
Supplement information for decision-making.	Makes decisions on their own, with minimum human intervention.
Mostly utilized in sectors like customer service, health care, industries, etc.	Used mostly in security, finance, healthcare, retail, manufacturing, etc.

Cognitive AI: Use Case

Cognitive computing and artificial intelligence are technologies that rely on data to make decisions. But there are subtle differences between these two terms, and they can be found in their uses and applications.

Let us imagine a scenario wherein a person decides to change their career. The AI assistant will automatically evaluate the skills of job applicants, find relevant jobs where their skills match the position, and negotiate salary and benefits. At the closing stage, it will make a decision for him and inform him accordingly.

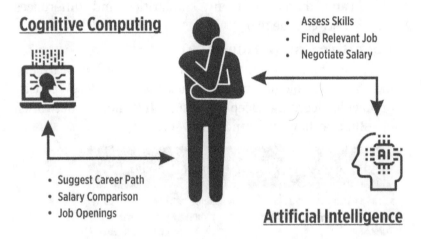

Cognitive Computing

- Assess Skills
- Find Relevant Job
- Negotiate Salary

- Suggest Career Path
- Salary Comparison
- Job Openings

Artificial Intelligence

- Cognitive assistants will suggest potential career paths to job applicants, in addition to providing them with some basic details, such as additional educational requirements, salary comparison data, and vacant positions. However, in this case, job seekers must still make a final decision.
- Cognitive computing helps you make smarter decisions, while AI suggests that machines can make better decisions for humans.

Applications of Cognitive AI

- **Smart IoT:** This includes connecting and optimizing devices, data, and the Internet of Things. However, assuming you have more sensors and devices, the real key is to connect them.
- **AI-Enabled Cybersecurity:** You can use data security encryption and AI-enhanced situational awareness to deal with cyber-attacks. This will provide a document, data, and network locking using smart distributed data secured by an AI key.
- **Content AI:** The solution supported by cognitive intelligence can continuously learn and reason, and can simultaneously integrate location, time of day, user habits, semantic strength, intention, emotion, social media, context awareness, and other personal attributes.
- **Cognitive Analytics:** The technology carries out human-like reasoning software functions that conduct deductive, inductive, and abductive analysis for life sciences applications.
- **Intent-Based NLP:** Cognitive intelligence can help companies conduct more analysis of management and decision-making methods. This will be the next step in machine learning, and future applications of artificial intelligence will rely on this to perform logical reasoning and analysis.

Relative Terminologies of AI

As a business leader, you should at least have a broad understanding of key Artificial Intelligence terminologies. This will help you to discuss with experts in the same language, and at the same time, you will also understand and map the requirement easily. Many different terms often used interchangeably; let's dive into the most common terminologies first.

Text Analytics

Text analysis can convert unstructured text data into meaningful data for analysis; to measure consumer opinions, product reviews, sentimental analysis, feedback to facilitate search facility and entity modeling to guide fact-based decision making. Text analytics uses algorithms to convert freeform text into data that may be analyzed via statistical, machine learning, and natural language processing techniques. Text Analytics involves data retrieval from unstructured data; data structuring so the input text derives patterns and trends, evaluation, and interpretation of the output data. It also includes lexical analysis, clustering, categorization, pattern recognition, tagging, annotation, fact extraction, link and affiliation analysis, visualization, and predictive analytics. Text Analytics determines keywords, topics, categories, semantics, tags from the millions of text data available in a company in different files and formats. Text Analytics is also called text mining.

The need for text analytics

Emails, online comments, tweets, call center agent descriptions, survey results, and other forms of written feedback can provide customers with insights. There is also a wealth of data in recorded interactions that can, without difficulty, be turned into a text. Text analytics unlocks meaning from the unstructured textual content. It lets you find patterns and themes, so you understand what clients are thinking about. It shows their wants and needs. Text analysis software programs can also provide early failure warnings by pointing out what customers are complaining about. Using text analytics tools, you can obtain valuable information from data that cannot be quantified in any other way. It turns the unstructured customer perspective into structured records that may be used by the business.

How Text Mining Works?

Text mining integrates concepts from different fields like linguistics and statistics, and Information and Communication Technologies (ICT). Statistical pattern learning constructs patterns from the extracted text. These patterns are analyzed to pull high-value insights. The process of text mining involves fact retrieval, lexical analysis, pattern recognition, tagging, fact extraction, data mining, and predictive analytics. In a way, text mining is summarized as,

Text mining = Lexicometry** + Data mining

The process starts with facts retrieval. A set of textual material is collected and identified. This can be from a website, database, document, or content management system. Parsing and other linguistic analysis is implemented to identify text features like people, organizations, area names, stock ticker symbols, and abbreviations.

**Lexicometry or lexical statistics is the study of measuring the frequency of words in textual data.

Applications of Text Analytics
1. Sentiment Analysis
2. Search access to unstructured data
3. Email spam filters
4. Automated advertisement placement
5. Social media monitoring
6. Competitive intelligence
7. Enterprise business intelligence and data mining
8. E-Discovery records management
9. National security and intelligence
10. Scientific discovery, especially life sciences
11. Competitive intelligence

Text Analysis Process

Text mining is challenging because data on different media is mostly unstructured. The crucial steps for any text mining process include:

1. **Extracting the keyword:** Selecting the relevant and particular keywords for individual queries is the first step within the text analysis process. The content and the linkage patterns are then used for keyword searches as content pieces with the same keywords are frequently linked to each other. The keywords function as social network nodes and are helpful in clustering the text.

2. **Classifying and Clustering the Text:** Different algorithms classify text from the content. The nodes are labeled and classified. The classified text is then clustered based on similarity. The linkage structure plays an essential role in the way text is classed and clustered. Node labeling and content-based classification are vital techniques for getting accurate results.

3. **Identifying Patterns:** Trend analysis is based totally on the principle that clusters gathered at different instances can also have different concept distribution even if the content is identical. Therefore, these concepts are compared and grouped into the same or different subsets accordingly.

Software Used for Text Mining

Text mining involves both unstructured and structured data. Structured data is commonly organized within Spreadsheets, while unstructured data is compiled in the form of reviews and summaries. Text mining software explores themes, patterns, and insights buried in both kinds of data. Organizations rely much on software for different data mining applications. Some standard packages for text mining are:

SAS Text Miner:
Text mining system that contains automated boolean rule generation, term profiling, document theme discovery, and text importing. It presents a suite of textual content processing and analysis tools.

DiscoverText: It is a web-based collaborative text analytics system that allows academics, companies, and governments to schedule, fetch data from Twitter, import from SurveyMonkey, email, or a spreadsheet, search, filter, cluster, human-code, and machine-classify text.

PrediCX: Automated predictive analytics for text. No data scientists are needed to build accurate models.

OdinText Text Analytics: SaaS text analytics and research system that includes advanced statistics, linguistic sentiment, and social media monitoring tools. Etuma: Real-time, multi-language customer, and employee open-text feedback topic and topic-level sentiment categorization service.

MonkeyLearn: The AI platform can analyze text through machine learning and convert emails, tweets, surveys, or any text into actionable data.

Crimson Hexagon Platform: Cloud social media analytics software with text analysis that enables you to review conversations, select examples, and make group posts.

Keatext: Keatext AI platform interprets customers' written feedback across various channels to highlight customer experience insights.

AlchemyLanguage: APL's text analysis system provides companies with entity extraction, sentiment and sentiment analysis, keyword extraction, and other tools.

InMoment: Cloud-based solution that offers leadership board, employee communication, and employee loyalty modeling capabilities.

WordStat: Text mining tools can quickly extract themes and trends. The latest qualitative content analysis.

Medallia Text Analytics: Web-based text analytics software that includes root cause analysis, comments analysis, and text analysis in social feedback.

Text Analyzer: Text analyzing solution that enables companies to find frequently used phrases or words and count number of words or characters.

IBM SPSS Predictive Analytics Suite: It is used for data and text mining.

Textalyzer: An online text analysis tool.

TensorFlow

TensorFlow is an open-source deep-learning library developed by Google that is used to perform complex numerical operations and several other tasks to model deep learning models. Its architecture allows easy deployment of computations across multiple platforms like CPU's, GPU's, etc. The products of the Google Brain team are used in Google Photos, Google Search, and Google Cloud Speech.

Characteristics TensorFlow

- It includes efficient C++ implementation of machine learning and custom C++ operations.
- High-level APIs such as TF Layers, Keras, and Pretty Tensor can run on top of TensorFlow. It provides a simple API TF-Slim (tensorflow.contrib.slim) for simple training routines.
- It can run on operating systems such as Windows, Linux and macOS, and mobile operating systems such as Android and iOS.
- It provides quite a few optimization nodes to search for parameters that minimize the cost function.
- It automatically calculates the gradient of the cost function. This is called Autodiff (automatic differentiating).

- It provides a visualization tool called TensorBoard, where you can view the calculation graph, learning curve, and many more.
- It provides a Python API called TF. Learning (*tensorflow.contrib.learn*) uses a few lines of code to train a neural network.

Types of APIs

The two main APIs provided by TensorFlow are:

1. TensorFlow Core API-low-level machine learning development
2. Higher Level APIs - more compact API, such as tf.layers or tf.contrib.learn

TensorFlow core API

TensorFlow core provides comprehensive programming control. It is best suited for machine learning researchers and others who need fine level control over their models.

Higher-level API

A higher-level API is built on TensorFlow Core. These are easier to learn and use than TensorFlow Core. They make repetitive tasks more comfortable and consistent among different users. Higher-level APIs such as *tf.contrib* learning can help you manage data sets, estimates, training, and inference.

What are Tensors?

Tensors are the input and output of TensorFlow or multidimensional data arrays. They are a set of values that are shaped into n-dimensional arrays with static and dynamic type dimensions. They represent physical entities mathematically, characterized by amplitude and multiple directions. They usually contain floating-point numbers, but they can also carry strings in the form of byte arrays. They can be passed between nodes of the computation graph and have data types. NumPy is a Python API for numerical calculations.

Tensor Ranks

In the TensorFlow system, tensors are defined by dimensional units called ranks. Tensor rank is not similar to matrix rank. Tensor rank (also referred to as *order* or *degree* or *n-dimension*) is the number of dimensions of the tensor. The dimensions of tensors can be described using levels, shapes, and dimensions. The shape and size of the tensor determine its grade. Other libraries perform deep learning with almost similar capabilities, but, Google's TensorFlow has proven to be a scalable, clean, flexible, and efficient. As Google backs, it has risen to the top of the developers' choice.

TensorFlow benefits

The most significant benefit TensorFlow provides for machine learning development is an abstract concept. Developers don't usually handle any specific details and can focus on the overall logic of the application. They can also set aside the worries of dealing with the implementation hassles of the algorithms. They are also not worried about finding out the correct method to connect the output of one function to the input of another function. TensorFlow takes care of the information in the back of the scenes.

TensorFlow provides more convenience for developers who need to debug and introspect TensorFlow applications. The desired execution mode allows you to transparently evaluate and modify each graphic operation separately instead of constructing the entire graphic as a single opaque object and immediately evaluating it. The TensorBoard visualization kit allows you to examine and analyze the way graphics are run through an interactive web-based dashboard.

TensorFlow has also gained numerous advantages from its association with Google. Google not only promoted the rapid development of the project but also developed many important products around TensorFlow, making them easier to deploy and use: the TPU as mentioned earlier, silicon for accelerated performance in Google's cloud; an online center for sharing models created using frameworks; browsers and mobile-friendly framework applications; and more.

One caveat: The implementation of TensorFlow makes it difficult for certain training jobs to obtain certain model training results. Sometimes the model trained on one system is slightly different from the model trained on another system, even if they are provided with the same data. The reason for this deviation is subtle. How and where to seed random numbers and, are there non-deterministic behavior when using GPUs? In other words, these problems can be solved, and the TensorFlow team is considering using more controls to influence the certainty in the workflow.

TensorFlow vs. the competition

TensorFlow competes with many other machine learning frameworks. PyTorch, CNTK, and MXNet are three important frameworks that meet many of the same needs. Few of the frameworks are:

PyTorch: In addition to building with Python, PyTorch has many other similarities with TensorFlow, including hardware acceleration components under the hood, a highly interactive development model that allows you to design on-demand, and contains many useful components. For the rapid development of projects that need to be up and running in a short period, PyTorch is usually the better choice, but TensorFlow wins over large projects and more complex workflows.

CNTK: CNTK is a Microsoft cognitive toolkit such as TensorFlow. It uses a graph structure to describe the data flow, but it focuses on creating deep learning neural networks. CNTK can process many neural network jobs faster and has a broader API set (Python, C++, C#, Java). However, CNTK is currently not as easy to learn or deploy as TensorFlow.

Apache MXNet: The Apache MXNet used by Amazon as the main deep learning framework on AWS, can scale linearly across multiple GPUs and multiple machines. It also supports various language APIs (Python, C++, Scala, R, JavaScript, Julia, Perl, and Go), although its native API is not as good as TensorFlow.

TensorFlow is most suitable for:

- Large Dataset
- High Performance
- Functionality
- Object Detection

Keras

Keras is nothing but an advanced neural network API that is written in Theano, CNTK, or Python. Designed to be able to use deep neural networks for rapid experiments, it focuses on becoming a user-friendly, modular, and scalable network. Its development focuses on rapid experiments and is part of the research work of ONEIROS (Open-ended Neural Electronic Intelligent Robot Operating System) project. Its author is the Google engineer François Chollet who also maintains it. Chollet is also the author of the XCeption deep neural network model.

Keras' Features

- Neural networks API
- Easy and fast prototyping
- Convolutional networks support
- Recurrent networks support
- Runs on GPU

Keras Alternatives

PyTorch

PyTorch is an open-source machine learning library based on the Torch library, used for applications such as computer vision and natural language processing, mainly developed by Facebook's AI Research Lab (FAIR).

TensorFlow

TensorFlow is an open-source software library for numerical calculations using data flow graphs. The nodes in the graph represent mathematical operations, and the edges of the graph represent multidimensional data arrays (tensors) that communicate between them. The flexible architecture of TensorFlow allows you to deploy computation to either one or more GPUs or CPUs in a server or on your mobile device, desktop, even with a single API.

Scikit-learn

Scikit-learn is a module of Python for machine learning, built on SciPy, and distributed under the 3-Clause BSD license.

ML Kit

ML Kit brings Google's machine learning expertise to mobile developers in a powerful and easy-to-use package.

CUDA

CUDA is a parallel computing platform and programming model developed by Nvidia, which enables developers to use the functions of GPU to realize the parallelizable part of the calculation, thereby accelerating the speed of computationally intensive applications.

Keras is most suitable for:

- Rapid Prototyping
- Small Dataset
- Multiple back-end support

Time series

Time series is nothing but the arrangement of statistical data in chronological order following time. A time-series offers the relationship between two variables: one of them is time. Mathematically, it is given by

Y = f(t)

Where "y" is the phenomena at any given time "t." Thus "y" can be taken as a feature of "t."

Time series components:

Trend: Increase or decrease a series of data over a more extended period.

Seasonality: The pattern fluctuations caused by seasonal determinants in the short term.

Cyclicity: Variations taking place at irregular intervals because of specific circumstances.

Irregularity: Instability due to random factors that are not repeated in the pattern. The primary concern of time series analysis is to study the net-effect of these components on the movement of the time series and also to study these components independently.

The number one concern of time series analysis is to examine the net effect of these components on the movement of the time series and also to look at these components independently.

Time series uses:

A time-series has profound importance in enterprises and policymaking. It is used:

1. To observe the past behavior of the phenomena under consideration.
2. Compare current trends with past or expected trends. Therefore, it clearly shows growth or decline.
3. In forecasting and policy planning by various organizations.
4. Cyclic changes help us understand the business cycle.
5. The seasonal variations are useful for businesses and retailers as they earn more in certain seasons. For example, a seller of clothes will make more profit if he sells woolen clothes in winter and silk clothes in summer.

Time Series Application:

Time series analysis can be used for a variety of purposes, such as:

- Stock Market Analysis
- Economic Forecasting
- Inventory Studies
- Budgetary Analysis
- Census Analysis
- Yield Projection
- Sales Forecasting and more.

Time Series Modeling

It involves data based on time (year, day, hour, minute) to draw hidden insights to make informed decisions. Time series models are very useful models when you have data related to a series. Most companies use time-series data to analyze next year's sales, website visits, competitive position, etc.

Few of the Time Series models are:

ARIMA Model

ARIMA (Autoregressive Integrated Moving Average version), that's a sort of regression analysis that measures the influence of one established variable on the changing variables. The model is used to forecast moves inside the economic market, analyze the differences in values in a collection compared to the actual values. ARIMA can be classified into three components:

- **AR**(Autoregression), where the dependent relationship is used between observation and many lagged observations.
- **I** (Integrated), where raw observation is differentiated and is used to make the time series stationary.
- **MA** (Moving Average), uses the dependency between observation and residual error. Every component is defined as a parameter which is replaced as integer to indicate the usage of the ARIMA model.

ARIMA and Stationarity

A stationary model consists of consistent data over a period. ARIMA model makes the data stationary through differencing. For instance, most of the economic data reflects a trend. Differencing of data eliminates the trends to make it stationary.

Below is an example of index values that are analyzed month-to-month. The plot shows an upward trend which has non-stationary data. Thus, the ARIMA model can analyze, predict, and make the data stationary:

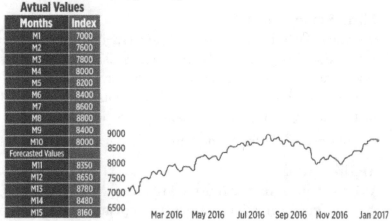

Avtual Values

Months	Index
M1	7000
M2	7600
M3	7800
M4	8000
M5	8200
M6	8400
M7	8600
M8	8800
M9	8400
M10	8000
Forecasted Values	
M11	8350
M12	8650
M13	8780
M14	8480
M15	8160

Source: ElegantJ BI

Autoregressive Model (AR)

The Autoregressive (AR) model derives the behavioral pattern from the past data to forecast the future. It is beneficial when there's a correlation among the data in a time series. The model is based on the linear regression of the data in the current time series relative to previous data on the same series.

The following is an example of the Google stock price from February 7, 2005, to July 7, 2005, with an n value of 105. Analyze the data to identify the AR model. In the figure below, the figure shows the relationship between stock price and time.

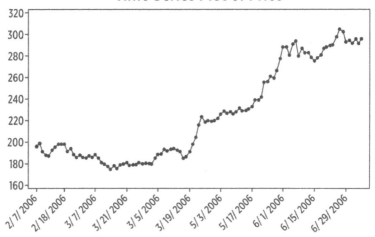

Time Series Plot of Price

Source: https://morioh.com/p/5d5c6c01f9e6

These values are closely related to each other, indicating that an AR model is needed. The following figure shows some autocorrelation of data:

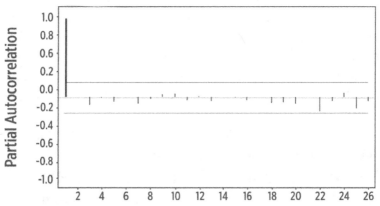

Partial Autocorrelation Function for price
(with 5% significance limits for the partial autocorrelations

Source: PennState

You can generate a lag-1 price variable and compare the scatter plot with the lag-1 variable:

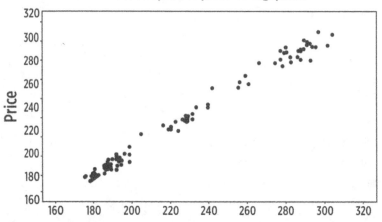

Scatterplot of price vs lag1price

Source: PennState

A moderate linear pattern can be observed, which indicates the suitability of the first-order AR model.

Moving Average Model (MA)

The moving average model is used to model a univariate time series. The model defines that the output variables are linearly related to the current and past data of the time series. It uses past errors in predictions in regression instead of the previous values of predictors. Moving averages help reduce "noise" in prices. If the moving average is sloping upwards in the chart, it means that the price has risen. If it points down, it means that the price is falling, and if the price moves sideways, the price is likely to be in the range.

In a 50-, 100-, or 200-day uptrend, the moving average may support the bottom line of a price rebound.

Natural Language Processing (NLP)

Natural language processing (NLP) is a branch of AI that can help computers understand, interpret, and manipulate human language. NLP lets developers organize and structure knowledge to perform tasks such as translation, summarization, named entity recognition, relationship extraction, speech recognition, and topic segmentation.

NLP is a way of computers to analyze, understand, and derive meaning from human languages such as English, Spanish, Mandarin, etc.

For Example, A robot is used to perform as per instructions. NLP system's input and output can be –

- Speech
- Written Text

NLP Techniques and Tools

Syntax and semantic analysis are the two main techniques used in natural language processing. Grammar is the arrangement of words in a sentence to facilitate grammatical understanding. NLP uses syntax to evaluate the meaning of language based on grammar rules. The syntax techniques used include parsing (grammatical analysis of sentences), word segmentation (dividing large sections of text into multiple units), sentence breaking (placement of sentence boundaries in large texts), morphological segmentation (dividing words into groups) and stemming (divide words with metamorphosis into root form).

Semantics involves the usage and meaning behind the word. NLP applies algorithms to understand the purpose and structure of sentences. The techniques used by NLP in conjunction with semantics include word sense disambiguation (which derives the meaning of a word based on context), named entity recognition (determining words that can be classified) and natural language generation (which will use a database to determine the semantics behind the word).

The current NLP method is based on deep learning, which is an AI that examines and uses patterns in the data to improve the understanding of the program. Deep learning models require large amounts of labeled data to train and recognize correlations, and assembling such large data sets is one of the main obstacles of current NLP.

The earlier NLP method involved a rule-based approach, in which a simpler machine learning algorithm was told which words and phrases to look for in the text and gave specific responses when these phrases appeared. But deep learning is a more flexible and intuitive method, in which the algorithm learns to identify the speaker's intent from many examples, just like how children learn human language.

NLP Tools

The three commonly used tools of NLP include NLTK, Gensim, and Intel NLP Architect.

- NTLK (Natural Language Toolkit) is an open-source python module with data sets and tutorials.
- Gensim is a Python library for subject modeling and document indexing.
- Intel NLP Architect is another Python library for deep learning topology and technology.

Components of NLP

There are two components of the Natural Language Processing systems:

a. Natural Language Understanding (NLU)

NLU can be used to learn the meaning of a text, and for this, you should understand the nature and structure of each word.

i. Lexical Ambiguity: - words have multiple meanings

ii. Syntactic Ambiguity: - the sentence with numerous parse trees.

iii. Semantic Ambiguity: - the sentence can have innumerable implications

iv. Anaphoric Ambiguity: - phrase or word have a different meaning.

b. Natural Language Generation (NLG)

You must produce meaningful phrases and sentences. This is the natural language form of internal representation. This process involves:

- **Text** Retrieve the relevant content from a knowledge base.
- **Sentence** Choose the required words for setting the tone of the sentence.
- **Text Realization:** Map sentence plan into sentence structure.

The NLU is harder than NLG.

Future of NLP

Human-readable natural language processing is the biggest AI-problem. It is almost the same as solving the central artificial intelligence problem and making the computer as intelligent as a human.

- With the help of NLP, future computers or machines will be able to learn from online information and apply it to the real world. However, a lot of work is required in this regard.
- Natural language toolbox or NLTK becomes more effective with natural language generation, and computers will become more capable of receiving and providing useful and resource-rich information or data.
- With the help of NLP, support for invisible UI, smarter search, intelligence from unstructured information, Intelligent Chatbot, and many more are becoming a reality.

- The idea of an invisible or zero user interface will depend on the direct interaction between the user and the machine, through voice, text, or a combination of the two. When applied to search, the same feature that enables chatbots to understand customer requests can enable the "search like you speak" feature (just like you can query Alexa) without having to focus on topics or keywords. Google has added NLP to Google Drive to allow users to search for documents and content in the conversational language.

Natural language vs. Computer Language

Parameter	Natural Language	Computer Languages
Ambiguity	Ambiguous in nature	Unambiguous
Redundancy	Employ lots of redundancy	Less redundant
Literalness	Made of idioms and metaphors	Mean exactly what they want to say

Natural Language Processing — Terminologies

a. **Phonology**: - A study of organizing sound.

b. **Morphology**: - A study of the construction of words from primitive meaningful units.

c. **Morpheme:** *A primitive unit of meaning in a language.*

- **Syntax:** Arrange words to make a sentence. It also involves determining the structural role of words in the sentence and phrases.
- **Semantics:** Defines the meaning of words. How you can combine words into expressive phrases and sentences.
- **Pragmatics:** Deals with the use and understanding of sentences in different situations. It also defines how the interpretation of the sentence is affected.
- **World Knowledge:** Includes general knowledge about the world.

Steps in NLP

Natural language processing usually includes five steps:

a. Lexical Analysis: It helps in analyzing the structure of words. A language's lexicon is the combination of words and phrases in it.

b. Syntactic Analysis (Parsing)

Parsing for the analysis of the word and arranging words in a particular manner that shows the relationship between words.

c. Semantic Analysis

The purpose of semantic analysis is to draw the exact meaning or meaning of the dictionary from the text. The job of the semantic analyzer is to check whether the text is meaningful.

d. Discourse Integration

The meaning of any sentence depends on the context in the previous sentence. It brings sense to immediately succeeding sentence.

e. Pragmatic Analysis

You are interpreting data for actual meaning, although you must derive the linguistic aspects that require real-world knowledge.

Use Cases of NLP

In simple terms, NLP represents automated dealing with natural human languages like speech or text. Although the idea itself is fascinating, the actual value behind it comes from the use cases.

NLP assists you with lots of tasks, and the fields of application just appear to grow daily. Here are a few examples:

- NLP facilitates the recognition and prediction of illnesses based on electronic health records and the patient's search. It can detect many health conditions from cardiovascular diseases to depression or even schizophrenia. For instance, Amazon Comprehend Medical is a service that uses NLP to extract sickness, medications, and treatment results from clinical trial reports, patient notes, and other electronic health records.

- Organizations can determine customer reviews of services or products by identifying and extracting information such as social media. This sentiment analysis can provide plenty of facts about customers' choices and their decision-making motivation.

- An inventor at IBM built a cognitive assistant that works like a customized search engine by collecting all information about you and then remind you of a name, a song, or anything you couldn't recall the instant you want to.

- Companies such as Yahoo and Google use NLP to filter and classify emails by analyzing the text in emails flowing through the server and blocking spams before it even enters your inbox.

- To help identify the fake news, the MIT NLP team has developed a new system to determine whether the source of the news is accurate or politically biased, and thus to test whether the news source can be trusted.

- Apple's Siri and Amazon's Alexa are examples of smart voice-driven interfaces that use NLP to respond to voice prompts and perform various operations, such as finding a specific store, telling us the weather forecast, suggesting the best office route, or turn on the lights at home.

- Having an insight into what is happening and what human beings are talking about can be very valuable to financial traders. NLP is used to track information, reports, remarks about possible mergers among companies; the whole thing can then be included in a trading algorithm to generate big profits. Remember: buy the rumor, sell the news.

- NLP is also used in the search and selection phase of talent recruitment to determine the skills of potential employees and even discover potential customers before they are active in the job market.
- Powered by IBM Watson, NLP technology, LegalMation, developed a platform to automate routine litigation tasks and help the legal team save time, cut expenses, and move strategic focus.

NLP is predominantly booming in the healthcare industry. While medical institutions are increasingly adopting electronic health records, this technology is improving care services and disease diagnosis and reducing costs. Through enhanced clinical records, patients can be better understood and benefited through better healthcare. The purpose should be to optimize their experience, and several agencies are already working on this.

Advantages of NLP

- Users can get answers within seconds of any questions about any topic.
- The NLP system provides answers to questions in natural language.
- The NLP system provides accurate answers to questions without unnecessary or unwanted information.
- The accuracy of the answer increases with the amount of applicable information provided within the question.   NLP procedure allows computers to communicate with humans in   their language   and scales other language-related tasks.
- It allows users to perform more language-based data compared to a human being in a fatigue-free, unbiased, and consistent way.
- NLP process helps in building highly unstructured data sources

Disadvantages of NLP

- Complex query language – If the question is not clear or is ambiguous, the system may not be able to provide the correct answer.

- The system is only built for a single specific task; due to limited functions, it cannot adapt to new fields and problems.

- NLP system doesn't have a user interface or features that allow users to further interact with the system.

Computer Vision (CV)

Prof. Fei-Fei Li defines computer vision as "a subset of mainstream artificial intelligence that deals with the science of making computers or machines visually enabled, i.e., they can analyze and understand an image."

Computer vision (CV) is a process (and a branch of computer science) that includes capturing, processing, and analyzing real-world photos and videos to allow machines to extract meaningful, contextual information from the physical world.

How Does Computer Vision Work?

In ML, computer vision is used for deep learning to study the data sets through annotated images that show an object of interest in the given image. Computer vision can understand the patterns and identify the visual data feeding thousands or millions of photos which have been categorized for supervised machine learning algorithms training. A simple example may be finding the edges in a photograph. You need to use a kernel to duplicate the differentiation function in the brightness values in the pixels and then set a threshold wherein the derivative is high - EDGES.

This necessitates the use of various software techniques and algorithms that enable the computers to establish patterns in all elements related to the labels and make accurate future predictions. Computer vision can be utilized most effectively by conducting image processing through machine learning. Computer vision leads to pattern recognition, detecting shapes, etc.

How is Computer Vision Different from Image Processing?

Both are parts of AI technology and are used for processing the data and building a model. Computer vision differs from image processing as it facilitates high-level information from photos or videos.

In computer vision, an image or video is used as input, and the goal is to understand (including being able to infer something about it) the image and its content. Computer vision uses image processing algorithms to solve some of its tasks. Computer Vision and picture processing are distinct. It deals with studying the picture - find the numerous compo nents within the photograph, find the edges, etc. It is a superior form of image processing wherein the input is an image, but the output isn't an image; it is an interpretation of the image.

The image process task includes filtering, edge detection, noise removal, and color processing. In complete processing, you receive an image as input and extract another image as an output that may be used to train the device via Computer Vision.

The predominant difference between Computer Vision and Image Processing is the goal (not the strategies used). For example, if the goal is to upgrade the image quality for later use, it is called image processing. If the aim is to visualize like people, detect defects, recognize objects, or automate driving, then it is referred to as Computer Vision.

Applications of Computer Vision

Computer vision core concepts are already being incorporated into every-day products.

CV in Self-Driving Cars

Computer vision permits self-driving vehicles to make sense of their surroundings. Cameras take videos from exclusive angles around the vehicle and feed it to the Computer Vision software, which then processes the pictures in real-time to find the extremities of roads, read traffic signs, find other cars, things, and pedestrians. The self-driving vehicle can then steer on streets and highways, avoiding barriers and safely driving its passengers to their destination.

CV in Facial Recognition

Computer Vision also performs a crucial function in facial recognition applications, the technology that allows computers to match photographs of humans' faces to their identities. Computer Vision algorithms identify facial features in pictures and compare them with databases of fake profiles. Consumer devices use facial recognition to verify the uniqueness of their owners. Social media apps use facial recognition to find and tag users. Law enforcement companies also depend upon facial recognition technology to pick out criminals in video feeds.

CV in Augmented Reality and Mixed Reality

Computer Vision plays a crucial role in augmented and mixed reality, the technology that permits computing gadgets like smartphones, tablets, and smart glasses to superimpose and embed virtual items on real-world imagery. Using Computer Vision, AR equipment detects objects in the real world to decide the places on a device's display to place a digital object. For instance, Computer Vision algorithms can assist AR applications to locate planes like tabletops, walls, and floors, by establishing depth and dimensions and placing virtual gadgets in the physical world.

CV in Healthcare

Health-tech has witnessed some excellent benefits of computers. With the help of computer vision algorithms, its algorithms can help automate tasks such as finding symptoms in x-ray and MRI scans or detecting cancerous moles in skin photos.

Challenges of Computer Vision

Inventing the machine that sees as a human does is a deceptively tricky assignment, not just because it's hard to make computer systems do it, but because you don't know how human vision works.

Studying biological vision needs an understanding of the perception of the organs like eyes, and also the interpretation of that perception within the brain. Much development has been made, both in charting the procedure and discovering the tricks and shortcuts utilized by the system. But like any other brain-related study, there is a long way to go.

Computer Vision Tasks

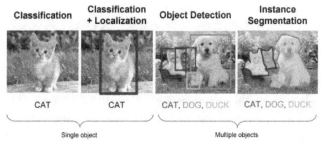

Source: Mike Tamir

Numerous renowned computer vision applications involve identifying things in photographs. In a picture Computer Vision involves object:

- **Classification**: The broad category of the object
- **Identification**: What is the object like?
- **Verification**: Can you see the object in the photograph?
- **Detection**: Where did you locate the object?

- **Landmark Detection**: Any critical points to detect the object.
- **Segmentation**: The pixels in the object.
- **Recognition**: What objects are there, and where are they?

Outside of just recognition, other methods of analysis include:

- With computer vision, video motion analysis can estimate the speed of objects in a video, or the camera itself.
- With image segmentation, algorithms separate images into many sets of views.
- A 3D model of a scene inputted through images or videos is created with scene reconstruction.
- With image restoration, noise (like blurring) is removed from photos using ML-based filters.
- Any other application that involves understanding pixels through software can safely be labeled as Computer Vision.

How to Choose the Model

The models need to be accurately selected to get correct results. To select the model, clear objectives like "What are you forecasting? What are the success parameters? What is then forecast horizon?" must be known.

The subsequent step is to research if the dataset is stationary or has a steady variable over-time or non-stationary. This helps in identifying the correct forecasting model.

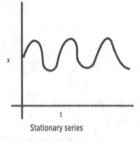

Stationary series

Non-Stationary series

Source: Datalytyx

The process leads to accurate analysis predicting the statistical properties relating to the past.

Chapter 4

Enterprise AI Strategy

****

"AI will create jobs, not kill them."

- Jeff Bezos, Amazon

****

While numerous leaders think that AI is critical and should be a crucial element in their competitive strategy, it is only about 8% of the organizations are engaged in the practices that support AI adoption. Many believe that it will change the level/nature of competition among industries and help to create new categories of products, markets, and business models. Leaders have the impression of falling behind and are thinking of implementing AI to get the desired outcomes with proper strategy.

AI Strategy

AI strategy is a plan for the implementation and execution of artificial intelligence, machine learning, or deep learning technologies in your organization. An AI strategy includes AI mission and vision, AI priorities, goals, and milestones of your organization. In summary, AI strategy is blending AI and strategy to get desired results. It focuses on AI implementation goals while business strategy focuses on the execution of corporate goals.

AI strategy options

When implementing AI in the organization, leaders should carefully think about the B2P (Build; Buy; Partner) options before they take any final decision. The confusion of whether to develop AI technologies or buy software perplexes most enterprises, from the smallest companies to the most significant industry leaders. Making the incorrect choice can be costly to innovation, market share, speed to the market, and more.

Build- Building AI applications within an organization implies developing the core AI solution with internal capabilities. For instance, when a healthcare company decides to develop applications to predict certain diseases – there could be two ways to go about it. Either to search the in-house talent pool to find an AI professional or a data scientist or to hire them externally.

Buy- Most of the car producers do not make every element themselves. Instead, they emphasize on areas where they can add more value while procuring other components from the expert organization. A similar approach can be taken with AI, for instance, buying software, APIs, or using open-source code. All software, and APIs, can be integrated into the business so they can develop another solution when technology advances.

Partner- With AI resources being scarce, organizations have trouble sourcing the right AI talent implying there is no skilled AI talent to develop useful applications. While organizations are hesitating to invest in expert talent before the value of AI has been demonstrated, some organizations have developed relevant competencies or services. Partnering with such organizations that have both domain knowledge and technical expertise would speed up AI application development.

Organizations often lean first toward the build option, because they believe they can maximize control over what is expected to be a competitive advantage. Sometimes it makes more sense to buy or partner. For example, small businesses often use APIs to access data from companies such as payment gateways in credit/debit card transactions, which can be used in AI solutions as well. If the required data or expertise does not exist internally, companies need to determine who they can partner with to obtain them quickly. These inputs may not be necessary for the entire solution, but they can significantly speed up their execution.

Leaders should also consider the following points before deciding to Build, Buy, or Partner.

1. **Feasibility:** A small POC will help understand the suitability and viability of the AI project. AI teams should be able to find and deliver use cases that demonstrate project viability in a shorter period. Use cases should be collected from different business units of the organizations for quick evaluation and prioritization, or cancelation if necessary. Discarding a business case that is not aligned with the business objectives is an excellent strategy.

A comprehensive feasibility study should help determine that if you don't understand the business case, it may cause the time and costs spent on the project to exceed expectations significantly, and ultimately lead to the disillusion of the technology. Moreover, an inability to make quick decisions may block the pipeline of AI plans, stifle potentially useful AI plans, and lead to the marginalization of other projects that may repeat work and lack reusability. A feasibility study should help determine the availability of off-the-shelf solutions or services that provide the required functional depth, at a cost much lower than the cost of building internal functions.

2. Organizational fit: AI project should be demand-driven. The value it will deliver should have crystal clear objectives and benefit (marginal or transformational), to understand the organizational fit. The project objectives should be aligned entirely with the business, and the stakeholders need to be committed and supportive in terms of backing decisions, internal resource allocation, internal communication, and flexibility.

3. Data: Stakeholders should know, "Is the data required for the intended purposes of the project available? Is that data unique?" If the project is using data generated internally as a part of the business model, does it have a higher probability of achieving success? If data or algorithms can be monetized, it will make more sense to build AI products or services internally to retain intellectual property rights (IPR). If the project's data is widely available in the market (for example, data from Facebook or Instagram or any other social media), then the company should consider purchasing its AI solution from outside. Considering there are many options, and the price is relatively low, companies can use "good enough" solutions without collecting their data and slowing the AI implementation process.

4. Strategic impact: Leaders should think, "Is the project strategic?" When a project brings a competitive advantage or a transformative impact, it has strategic importance. If the objectives are narrow (let's say, to keep pace with competitors or meet customer expectations), the impact of the project is more likely to be tactical.

In addition, stakeholders should consider whether the project is only relevant to the organization or only to the function of implementing it or whether the project is also useful to other parts of the business. Solutions or tools that can be easily adjusted and reused by multiple departments, or functions, are considered strategic, even if the development team is pursuing tactical business goals. An AI project with a strategic significance may well merit a decision to build internally; however, that would depend on the existing internal capabilities.

5. Capabilities: If the AI project is considered strategic, then stakeholders should analyze whether the organization has internal capabilities to deliver it. If the answer is yes, then internal development usually makes sense. If speed is critical, and existing internal resources cannot be used immediately, then a vendor solution or partner will be beneficial.

Leaders may also consider acquiring a start-up with the right solution, and ready-made capabilities could also be a good option. If the organizations have trouble attracting and affording the right people—buying or partnering becomes an attractive option.

A mixed approach is also feasible, wherein companies can utilize partners or purchase off-the-shelf components (to ensure better results in a shorter period, while reducing risk), while simultaneously developing a capability that can take on the more substantial burden of future projects. However, in all cases, companies should always ensure that they do not reinvent commercialized products, which are available at a reasonable price in the market.

Note: *A project of tactical importance should almost always entail a buy or partner approach, given the lower costs and risks involved in pursuing these. However, answering the build-or-buy-or-partner question will always be a case-by-case decision.*

AI Operating Models

Organizations have different operating models, and as a result, the question of the strategic versus the tactical impact of an AI solution may be addressed differently.

Distributed: A highly decentralized way of working is a sign of mature technology, tools, and usage patterns. Here, data scientists have plenty of resources to use and can work productively in loose teams, using established reuse methods and providing knowledge and expertise for a broader range of businesses.

Centralized: In this, all data science and AI projects are executed centrally by a specialized team. If local groups want to use technology for all aspects of development, they need to consult the center. Although this model is useful, it may become a bottleneck for the company's value and growth, especially for large companies, where it is difficult to achieve this level of command and control.

Hub-and-spoke:
A central hub can help drive standards, methods, and tools and guide work priorities as the organization matures to support technology. It consists of people belonging to the hub (AI experts, data scientists, and engineers) and experts belonging to the business department.

Few organizations can create value by building AI capability internally. Leveraging existing solutions and capacities developed by other companies can often achieve the desired business results faster and more economically. To obtain similar results from the building, the organization will have to invest more time, money, and energy, which only makes sense when the project is a strategic difference for them. Therefore, the best method is to invest in two ways:

---

1. Go to the market quickly by integrating what already exists. Take advantage of the innovation wave and the investment of others.
2. Invest in internal capabilities to create long-term value and differentiation by building something that will support the upcoming business.

This basic approach will maximize the value that organizations get from AI and reduce wasting time, effort, and resources.

Adopting an enterprise AI strategy enables and empowers businesses of any size to improve a single or multiple workforce function or business process. For example, artificial intelligence-enabled chatbots that handle interactions between customers and customer service executives or sales executives free up much of the employees' time, enabling them to be more productive somewhere else. This also allows employees to focus on the core business functions targeted at growing business revenues and scale. Data management is one of the core business functions that artificial intelligence software solves with a high degree of accuracy and speed, drastically enhancing productivity.

Regardless of the industry, enterprise AI has the potential to cover almost every business function and improve the efficiencies and effectiveness of business processes. Similarly, enterprise AI solutions form a part of the core offerings of many businesses nowadays. The list below denotes some of the many business functions wherein enterprise AI solutions play a critical role:

- Statutory Compliance and Legal affairs

- B2B Sales and Marketing.

- Business Intelligence

- Digital Commerce

- Finance and Operations

- Consumer Marketing

- Security and Risk.

- Customer Management

- Engineering and Internet Technology

- Data Science

- Industrial and Manufacturing

- Human Resources and Talent

- Logistics

- Productivity

It is evident from the list above that almost all business functions can be solved and enhanced with an enterprise AI strategy, provided that the right approach is chosen for the right business function. Some of the significant guidance areas in developing an enterprise AI strategy for your company are provided below:

Building AI Teams

An idea that will crop-up multiple times in this book is the importance of AI and machine learning teams in any business, involved in tech that is interested in getting the most out of artificial intelligence. Building AI teams allows businesses to use artificial intelligence innovatively and oversee their use as per legal and ethical compliance. Although many governments have not yet enacted legislation forcing companies to regulate the behavior of their AI, this is something looming on the horizon. Businesses can use AI teams for this function and circumvent future problems, which can cost them millions in fines and fees.

But building an AI team requires some thought about how the team should be constructed. How many members should there be on the team? What sort of background should team members have? What sorts of functions will its members perform? There is a lot of Al talent out there, and enlisting this talent means thinking about both your Al needs and what the talented individuals could potentially contribute to your business.

In terms of AI team structure, small teams headed by C-suite executives like chief information officer or a chief AI officer will be well-suited to be engaged in testing Al programs. Research suggests that such teams should have their budget, so they are not constrained by the financial concerns that can slow down the pace of activities of business units and lead to inefficiency and lethargy. It is also essential that these teams have access to other members of the C-suite and business leaders, which allows them to act fast to provide direct benefit to the company both in innovation and problem-solving.

Teams can be structured with a variety of professionals based on the function and needs of the business. Depending on the role of the Al, it is common for machine learning and other AI teams to have data scientists, machine learning engineers, data engineers, applied scientists, and other scientists. For example, AI involved in agriculture using heavy machinery might require agricultural scientists or biologists who are knowledgeable about the less obvious implications of the AI, such as the impact on humans and the environment from the Al automation or augmentation.

Use of AI in Multiple Projects
A crucial aspect of an enterprise AI strategy is the use of artificial intelligence in multiple projects rather than focusing on single-use AI that is less integrated. This allows AI technology to take full advantage of the company's data. It also makes use of the power of the artificial neural networks of deep learning, enabling AI to perform multiple complex

---

operations with data, akin to how human beings use information in various ways rather than just one.

As an example, Al can be used in multiple functions in industries like heavy machinery, manufacturing, or agriculture. In heavy industries, AI can be used in equipment monitoring, site monitoring, and employee safety, allowing the business to automate tasks that may be mandated by law. In agriculture, artificial intelligence may be involved in weed control, analysis of images from satellite or drones, to augmentation of automated equipment. Again, Al teams should have strong knowledge of the multiple roles of AI, allowing them to monitor the AI performance adequately.

Teams with Knowledge of Modeling

It is important to stress how critical it is to have individuals on staff who understand Al well enough to assist in the development (and maintenance) of the company's Al strategy. As you may be well aware at this point, machine learning algorithms involve the construction of mathematical models that link inputs to outputs. AI teams need to be knowledgeable about modeling to supervise or oversee these tasks. You also need to understand how AI works with composters and how AI functions may improve (or even take unpredicted directions) with deep learning.

AI-Ready Culture

You may have brilliant ideas for using artificial intelligence to improve organizations and communities, but turning these ideas into workable software requires the right mindset, the right skills, professional leadership, and a diverse support team.

Know Your Readiness

Despite many public claims for innovations, many companies are still catching up with existing technologies, such as big data, mobile, and Internet of Things (IoT). Many brands have established their own social media profile, and now offer mobile-apps and websites. Still, these are just digital consumer endpoints, not the foundation of enterprise-wide technological transformation. Other companies have accumulated large amounts of data but have not actively converted their information assets into improved business practices.

Central Technology Infrastructure and Technology Team

A crucial milestone in the corporate digital transformation is the development of a centralized data and technology infrastructure. These two elements connect consumer applications, enterprise systems, and third-party partners and provide access to a single source of truth that contains relevant, up-to-date, and accurate information for all parties. Designing and implementing the infrastructure needed for enterprise-scale AI requires a dedicated and robust technology team that can develop internal application programming interfaces (APIs) to standardize access to both data and your company's internal business technology. It will enable your company to streamline enterprise-wide data analysis, accelerate product development, and respond more quickly to evolving markets. Internal APIs will also reduce the communication overhead needed to hunt down specific data, negotiate access, and interpret variations. You will also avoid duplicating software development work across different departments that have overlapping needs and goals.

Non-technical companies usually prioritize technology as their second priority while leaving software projects to isolated business units. This can lead to technology flooding,

---

which indicates when different business units implement their own plans without consulting each other; build conflicting or incompatible solutions; compromise security due to inconsistent standards and access rights and; overload IT departments that struggle to monitor and manage all the burdens. If your company has not successfully managed the technical expansion (or you have not started to solve the problem), it is recommended to solve the problem before the start of a complex AI program.

If it can't be solved, the proliferation of technology will cause your company to invest in try-on and start-up or purchase third-party AI products for narrow purposes, which will only aggravate your existing problems. Establishing and maintaining a strategic, centralized, and secure architecture also requires a strong management commitment led by C-Suite, as well as continuous operational collaboration among all departments and business units.

Value Data and Analytics

If the analysis will be ignored, it makes no sense to collect data and run complex machine learning models laboriously. Historically, many of the world's largest companies have been developed through intuitive decision-making by influential executives, rather than through data-driven collaborative decision-making. Due to past success, some leaders prioritize their beliefs and methods and openly oppose analytical methods and centralized techniques.

During our professional careers, almost all of us have worked with colleagues with dogmatic qualities. They have a special name, HiPPO, which stands for the "highest-paid person's opinion." HiPPO insists that its strategy is the right direction for the company, which is mainly based on their ideas. Proposing new "visions" in the company, or shooting down initiatives that they perceive are competing with their agenda, executives who exhibit this behavior rarely mean being malicious, and do not recognize themselves as HiPPO, and prefer to refer themselves as being "experienced" or "visionary."

In the 15 years from 2002 to 2017, the top five listed companies by market value have moved from GE, Microsoft, Citi, and Wal-Mart to technology companies such as Apple, Alphabet, Microsoft, Amazon, and Facebook. Although data alone cannot make decisions for you, combining the right information with experience, creativity, and an unbiased perspective will enable executives to make better decisions.

Almost every company has a few executive HiPPOs. While you can probably manage a handful of naysayers, your company is unlikely to be competitive in AI if you're up against a HiPPO army or an extremely powerful C-Suite HiPPO. You have seen data and analytics initiatives at major companies severely hindered or even canceled by antagonistic executives.

Who should own AI initiatives?

One pattern stands out clearly: in every single tech firm that currently leads in AI, the CEO has come out strongly in favor of prioritizing AI company-wide.

Microsoft CEO Satya Nadella describes AI as being "at the intersection of our ambitions. You want to democratize AI just like you brought information to your fingertips".

Google CEO Sundar Pichai boldly said: "We will shift from mobile priority to the first world of AI."

Amazon's Jeff Bezos called modernity the "golden age" of AI. He said: "We are now solving the problems of machine learning and artificial intelligence in the realm of science fiction over the past few decades."

CEO, CTO, CIO, CDO, or CAO?

Finding the right stakeholders to support high-risk, high-return technology plans is half the battle. In companies that have traditionally been conservative about technology and digital investment, you may have difficulty persuading the CEO to support the AI program. In this case, try to find the highest possible management buy-in, preferably within C-Suite, or even at the board level.

Many different executives' roles can lead to successful enterprise AI applications, but leaders cannot rely solely on aspirational press releases. Vision, action, and budget must be used to prove true leadership skills. Executives should also have a high level of technical expertise, including the ability to understand or be willing to learn to develop data, analytics, machine learning products, and more.

The ideal characteristics of executive AI champions include: C-Suite executives or senior, business and domain experts, credible and influential, technical knowledge, analysis and data-driven, control sufficient budget, encourage experimentation, understand, and accept risks.

Key Stake Holders for AI initiatives

Chief Executive Officer (CEO)

In an ideal world, the CEO and the board of directors recognize the growing importance of AI and automation everywhere. As a result, they have empowered their executives with decision-making capability, financial budget, and organizational resources to succeed. More importantly, they are technology savvy enough to understand the risks involved and are committed to driving the progress.

CEOs of leading tech-based companies have realized the importance of AI for their businesses in the public and are committed to it. However, it has been found that even the CEOs from non-technology-based companies can get caught up with existing strategic initiatives and lose traction on AI efforts. While you should always strive to have your CEO's blessings, you may want to concentrate on finding a C-Suite champion who can dedicate a substantial amount of time to guide the AI investments to fruition.

Chief Technology Officer (CTO)

The chief technology officer creates technology for the company's external business or individual customers. The CTO defines the technical architecture, manages the engineering team, and continuously improves the technology behind the company's product line. Innovation, technical skills, and innovative capabilities are critical to the success of CTO.

As technology products increasingly rely on machine learning methods to improve performance, companies that primarily produce software will need their CTOs to prioritize investments in AI. Over the years, Google, Facebook, Amazon, Microsoft, and other large technology companies have prioritized integrating machine learning into their customer-facing products, as have leading companies in almost every field.

Chief Information Officer (CIO)

The chief information officer manages the technology and infrastructure that support the company's business operations. The chief information officer is responsible for the organization's IT and operations to simplify and support business processes. Unlike CTO, CIO's customers are internal users, functional departments, and business units. CIOs usually adapt and integrate third-party infrastructure solutions to meet unique business needs and have less custom development than CTO.

Because of the need to develop and integrate infrastructure to support AI, CIOs may play a vital role in implementing AI in organizations. ML systems and data mining systems require complex storage, network, and computing systems, which requires CIO's input to be realized in many enterprises. For non-technical companies, if the main benefit of adopting AI is to improve analysis and business operations, rather than affecting functions such as sales and marketing that affect external customers, then CIOs can be the right stakeholders.

Chief Data Officer (CDO)

As data touches all aspects of enterprises, Chief Data Officers are increasingly becoming common, but their mandate is more often the security, regulation, and governance of enterprise data. Depending on their focus, they typically report to CIOs, CFOs, Chief Risk Officers (CROs), or Chief Security Officers (CSOs). Companies that have the CDO report directly to the CEO tend to value data and analytics more highly than those that don't.

Once a CDO or comparable leader has organized high-quality data, one can apply meaningful analytics to solve business problems.

Other Significant Roles

The roles we emphasize are often those with sufficient technical expertise, organizational resources, and corporate influence to lead major AI initiatives. However, successful investments can be led by a variety of roles, including a chief digital officer, chief security officer/chief information security officer, chief risk officer, chief innovation officer, chief science officer, and chief strategy officer. The AI plan can also be led by the chief marketing officer (CMO), chief operating officer (COO), chief financial officer (CFO), or other corporate leaders. They have business decisions and maintain significant political influence within the organization.

Chief AI Officer (CAIO) "Like electricity transformed countless industries about 100 years ago, internet revolutionized the world similarly 25 years ago, now it is artificial intelligence about to bring the same revolution," writes Andrew Ng, former Stanford University Professor of Computer Science and a widely respected technical expert on machine learning. Just as the need for CIOs grew with the rise of the Internet and the demand for CDOs surged increasing

---

importance of data, Ng proposed that organizations establish a new role – the Chief AI Officer (CAIO) – to govern and champion the role of AI in enterprises.

Ng states the primary benefit of CAIOs is how they can centralize a powerful AI team that can build and use AI technology to accelerate and streamline business functions across an organization, not just in silos. "A dedicated AI team is more likely to attract AI talent and maintain standards."

Successful CAIOs not only need to master AI and data infrastructure technologies, but also must be able to collaborate with different departments and different roles effectively, understand their priorities when formulating business problem solutions, and have enough charm to win support for new initiatives, and have enough industry influence to attract highly sought-after talent to join their team.

Artificial intelligence is not a magic solution to solve all challenges in an instant. Usually, different, more straightforward methods can also drive many improvements and advances. Successful deployment of AI also requires your organization to "support AI," that is, a strong culture of data-driven decision-making and technical experimentation. Otherwise, even the best CAIOs in the world will not bring any benefit to your company.

Organizational Buy-In

Most AI implementations are cross-functional and require input from multiple departments. Updating your accounts payable system will require input from financial, legal, security, and technology departments. To succeed, you will need the support of other supervisors, first-line managers, and their employees. You can take the following measures to win the support you need from your organization.

Focus on Revenue Potential
A key strategy is to appeal to your business leaders about the potential of increasing the bottom line. AI can save time and energy, reduce costs, and increase profits, which then provide executives an opportunity to grow their business lines and advance their careers.

Stay Ahead of the Competition
The fear of missing out (FOMO) is also a powerful motivating force. If business unit leaders fail to take action, emphasize that they are setting themselves up to fall behind competitors who are jumping on new technology. Not investing in the organizational and technical requirements to adopt AI may mean falling so far behind that they're unable to compete in the future.

Start Small for Early Wins
Pick a smaller, sure-win project to demonstrate possibilities. While returns may be limited, an initial success will give you the required confidence when you request that the project scope be expanded. Aim for something with a short time horizon that can be completed with a small task force. For example, in customer care, nuance recommends routing a tiny portion of customer support queries to an AI system at the onset. Initially, an automated support system can answer 20 to 30 percent of frequently asked questions. Still, accuracy can increase to over 80 percent and expand to more topics as the system learns over time.

Fears of Job Loss Ousted
Considering the negative media hype surrounding AI, it is understandable that your employees may have been concerned about the safety of their job. You can eliminate these fears and promote a healthy working environment wherein people and machines work together and thrive. As per McKinsey (n.d.), 45 percent of tasks are automatable, only 5 percent of total work has been replaced by automation. The

artificial intelligence system mainly deals with a single task, not the entire job.

High costs, legal regulations, and social resistance to AI all hinder the progress of technology adoption. With the rise of autonomous vehicles, many believe that the jobs of America's 1.7 million truck drivers are in imminent danger. The reality is that trucking jobs will likely require many years to get replaced. Michael Chui, a McKinsey partner, told *The New York Times* that the replacement and retrofitting of America's truck fleet with autonomous navigation would require a trillion-dollar investment that few, if any, companies will immediately undertake. Even if financing can be secured, autonomous vehicle technology is not yet approved for industrial or for individual use.

If humans can outsource repetitive and mundane tasks to AI, they can devote more attention to tasks requiring strategic skills such as judgment, communication, and creative thinking. As employees engage in increasingly meaningful work, eliminating the boring jobs they don't like to do, they get a significant morale boost, and their interest grows. Accenture's operations department has more than 100,000 employees, and it initially calculated that automation would replace 17,000 jobs in its accounts payable and marketing operations. However, as employees moved to more strategic consulting services to expand their business scope, the number of employees increased.

The Internet and mobile technology revolution have created more jobs than it has destroyed. Artificial intelligence may have the same effect, but new opportunities in the digital economy will require superior technical skills and knowledge. Demonstrating your commitment to retrain your employees for changing roles and responsibilities will go a long way toward gaining their consent and trust.

Questions about AI to C-Suite executives

Boards will want to understand AI's opportunities and its risks. Here are some questions boards can ask C-level executives about how AI will fit into the company's strategy:

1. Have you considered how AI can transform your products or services and which aspects of your business could benefit from increased automation or machine learning?
2. How may AI fit with other emerging technologies you are investing in?
3. Do you have the computing power and infrastructure to support the use of AI? Do you have the digital skills and talent to move forward?
4. How will you gain the trust of your stakeholders if you use AI?
5. Have you thought about how you will use data collected by AI? Have you considered cyber risks and data privacy issues?

AI Strategy Framework

How do you decide which problems to resolve first with AI?

AI Strategy Framework provides a standard set of criteria for evaluating each opportunity. The weight of each factor will change depending on your business priorities.

Rationale: First, understand the project's strategic rationale. How does the opportunity fit into your company or department's overall goals and strategic plan? Decide whether this is a revenue-increasing or a cost-cutting measure. How might this change the products and services that your company offers? Will it open new business opportunities? Typically, opportunities are judged against a mid- to long-term time horizon.

Opportunity size: Consider the opportunity size. Is the opportunity big enough to warrant an AI solution, or can your employees or an older technology adequately solve the problem? Conversely, even if this specific opportunity can be solved more cheaply or easily with human power for now, can an AI-based solution be leveraged for similar tasks in the future?

Investment: Consider the investment level required. How much time and money will you need to allocate toward the problem? Don't forget to include internal costs. For example, even if an external vendor implements a solution, you will still incur internal management costs.

ROI: While the next factor, the return on investment (ROI), is never guaranteed, you should estimate an upper and lower benchmark and a likelihood of success. Understand your break-even number. Don't forget to include internal costs for project management and opportunity costs in your evaluation.

Risk: What is the likelihood that this project will succeed and deliver on the projected ROI? Does this project seem like a sure bet, or is it a moon-shot opportunity? Set the performance level that new technology needs to achieve to be deemed successful. Also, consider the industry risk of your competitors adopting AI for a core function. Would you lose your competitive advantage if you failed to take action?

Timeline: -Timeline is the next factor to consider. Most AI projects require at least a few months of investment before producing positive results for your business. During this period, you should always be optimizing and testing your technology. A project that takes many years to complete should set interim milestones to measure progress.

Finally, have other business stakeholders bought in? Most projects will require an interdepartmental effort to gather data, train systems, launch new products, and maintain performance.

Must-Haves for AI Strategy

Followings are the five "Must Haves" for every AI strategy: -

1. **Stakeholders Buy-in:** - support and agreement, financial inputs from stakeholders
2. **People skills:** – employees with right skillsets like engineers, analytics experts, and data scientists, (coding, ML, domain knowledge)
3. **High-quality data:** – attributable, accurate, accessible data
4. **Sample use case:** - start by finding a use case that is similar in size and consumes a lot of time (typically an administrative task) that no one likes to do.
5. **Start small:** - start small to gain successes then scale up.

When starting an AI project with a client, these five must-haves' go a long way toward increasing the probability of success from planning to implementation.

AI in action

Artificial intelligence is a constellation of technologies that allows machines to sense, comprehend, act, and learn to extend human capabilities. Organizations get the greatest value when humans and machines work together and complement each other's strengths.

Corporate feel high pressure to use AI, the potential of AI grows every day, and they want to avoid falling behind.

The success of AI is not guaranteed if AI-powered solutions will get implemented in a rush without a broader vision and strategy in place.

How to release the full power of AI? Here are some actions to be taken:

1. Understand the data
2. Organize the data
3. Make data actionable

AI plays a significant role in optimizing and making things more efficient, once data is actionable. It helps to build new disruptive ideas, and to conceptualize new ways of action, e.g., how can one use images and build a diagnostic application or how can one use data and develop conversational agent. A smart strategy is to steer data from the raw stage to the actionable stage quickly.

To transform your entire business, begin with a strong AI strategy that empowers you to invest in the right systems, build responsible practices, and prepare your business and people for tomorrow.

Chapter 5

The AI Economy Strategy

****

"Predicting the future isn't magic; it's artificial intelligence."

-Dave Waters

****

The AI Stakes Are Higher

Some AI-based services and tasks in the present world are relatively trivial – such as movie recommendations on Netflix. However, artificial intelligence is playing an increasingly important role in other fields and has a more significant impact on humans. Imagine the importance of AI-enabled applications in crises like Coronavirus (COVID-19). If you're a doctor using AI-enabled sensors to examine a patient, you need not be in direct contact with the patient, and still, you can treat patients with the help of AI-enabled applications.

AI will not replace people but will complement and support them so they can make better, faster, more accurate, and more consistent decisions. The development of an AI economy requires businesses to be smart in their AI development strategies. The AI strategies allow enterprises to incorporate AI into their operations effectively; use AI insights and predictions in ways that benefit the business; maintain and increase profits, and manage various enterprise issues.

Key Components for AI Business Strategies

The following is a list of the key components that business strategies in the artificial intelligence economy should have:

1. Efficient Use of Business Intelligence and Analytics
A business strategy that does not take account of business intelligence would be ineffective.

Business intelligence, the business information on workforce and other issues allow businesses to grow and evolve, and to adapt to changes. Artificial intelligence is used extensively in business intelligence as AI can be used to help enterprises to track data and understand data. This takes us back to the realms of predictive analytics and actionable analytics. Using valuable business data, AI can help provide the business with insights, and this is a core component of a solid business strategy in the AI economy.

2. Teaching AI to the C-suite
The chief officers of a business are necessary because they are often tasked with steering the business in the right direction in their areas of leadership and expertise. Many tech companies have a chief AI officer, or at the least, a chief intelligence officer, who can make AI understandable to business executives. But usually, businesses do not, which means that education of the C-suite about AI can be one of the most critical components of a business strategy in the tech economy. Although the AI economy means that business executives will find themselves working more closely with data and computer scientists, this does not absolve the C-suite of the responsibility of educating themselves about AI so they can make the best business decisions.

3. Management of AI Risk
AI is risky because of trust issues in public regarding AI, and because artificial intelligence still has problematic areas that can expose the business to problems later. Most of you will be familiar with these areas, as they have been discussed in the

---

previous chapters. The use of artificial intelligence can expose the business to security risks or issues of privacy issues. As governments become more aware of privacy issues surrounding web data, companies will have to address the problems of AI risk in their business strategies. This includes the obvious Band-Aid of machine learning teams or algorithmic monitoring teams, in addition to knowledgeable security departments that can handle these issues.

Mistakes and solutions

ML gives organizations the ability to make accurate data-driven decisions and solve the problems that have puzzled traditional analytical methods. However, ML is not magic. It poses challenges, like other analytics methods. The following are the major ML mistakes and their suggested solutions:

Mistake 1: Machine Learning Program Without Data Scientists

The shortage of in-depth analytics talent is still a severe challenge, and demand for employees who can manage and consume analytics content is even higher. Hiring and retaining these much-needed technical experts has become the focus of many organizations.

Data scientists are the most skilled analytics professionals and require a unique fusion of computer science, mathematics, and domain expertise. Experienced data scientists demand high salaries and attract large numbers of projects.

Steps to solve it: -

- Develop an Analytics Center of Excellence (DACOE): These centers act as analytical consulting within the organization. The center can bring analytical talent in one place and can effectively use the analytical skills of the entire enterprise.
- Collaborate with universities: Create an internship program or university recruitment plan to find new talent. You can also use university courses that pair students with industries.
- Cultivate talent from within: Search for employees who have natural math and problem-solving aptitude and invest in data science and ML training for them.
- Make analysis easier to get started: If your data visualization tool is user-friendly, and the data is easy to explore, then others in the business can also solve data problems, not just data scientists.

Mistake 2: Starting Without Quality Data

Although improved algorithms are often regarded as fascinating aspects of machine learning, the ugly fact is that most time is spent in preparing data and dealing with quality issues. Data quality is critical to obtain accurate results from the model. Some of the many data quality issues include:

- Noisy data: - Data that contains a lot of conflicting or misleading information
- Dirty data: - Data with missing values, categorical and character features with multiple levels, and inconsistent and incorrect values
- Sparse data: - The data contains very few actual values but mainly consists of zero or missing values
- Inadequate data: - The data is incomplete or biased.

Steps to solve it: -

- Data security and governance: Address data security problems at the beginning of machine learning exercises, especially if you need support from other departments. Similarly, initial plans for data governance should consider how to use, store, and reuse algorithms.
- Data integration and preparation. After collecting and cleaning, the data must be converted into a logical format that can be used by machine learning algorithms.
- Data exploration. Productive machine learning exercises should start with specific business needs and produce quantifiable results. Once machine learning models are trained, data scientists must have the ability to effectively query, summarize and visualize data, and build algorithms as new data is added.

Mistake 3: Inadequate Machine Learning Infrastructure

For most organizations, managing all aspects of the infrastructure surrounding machine learning activities can itself be a challenge. Trusted and reliable relational database management systems may be completely ineffective when organizations now seek to collect and analyze variety and large amounts of data.

Steps to solve it: -
Planning the following areas can ensure that your infrastructure can handle machine learning.

- **Flexible storage:** - Design an appropriate, organization-wide storage solution that meets data requirements and has room to mature with technology advances. Storage considerations should include data structure, digital footprint, and usage.

- **Robust computation:** - The powerful, scalable, and secure computing infrastructure enables data scientists to recuse multiple data preparation techniques and different models to find the best solution within a reasonable time
- **Hardware acceleration:** - Use SSD (solid-state drives) for I/O-intensive tasks such as data preparation or disk-enabled analytics software. For computationally intensive tasks that can run in parallel, such as matrix algebra, use a graphics processing unit (GPU).
- **Distributed computing:** - In distributed computing, data and tasks are split on many connected computers, which usually reduces execution time. Make sure that the distributed environment you use is ideal for machine learning.
- **Elasticity:** - The consumption of storage and computing resources may be highly dynamic in machine learning, requiring a lot of support in some time intervals and fewer resources at other time intervals. Infrastructure elasticity can make better use of limited computing resources and financial expenses.

Mistake 4: Too Early or No Strategy to Implement Machine Learning

Numerous data-driven organizations have spent years developing successful analytical platforms. Choosing when to incorporate newer and more complex modeling methods into the overall analytics strategy is a difficult task. Until IT and business needs evolve, it is not necessary to transition to machine learning technology. In regulated industries, the interpretation, documentation, and rationality of complex machine learning models add an additional burden.

Steps to solve it: -

Position machine learning as an extension of existing analytical processes and other decision-making tools. For instance, a bank may use traditional regression in its regulated transactions. Still, it will use more accurate machine learning techniques to predict when the regression model will become outdated and need to be refreshed. For organizations with ambitious business needs, several innovative technologies have proven effective:

- **Anomaly detection:** Although there is no one way to solve actual business problems, there are several machine learning algorithms known to enhance the detection of anomalies, outliers, and fraud.
- **Segmented model factories:** Sometimes, the market has very different market segments. In health care, every patient in the treatment group needs special attention. In these cases, applying different predictive models to each market segment or each patient may lead to more targeted and practical actions. Using the model factory method to build models across multiple market segments or individuals automatically can achieve improvement in efficiency and accuracy.
- **Ensemble models:** Compared to using a single model alone, combining the results of many models can produce better predictions. Although ensemble modeling algorithms (such as random forests, gradient boosting machines, and more) have shown great promise, custom combinations of pre-existing models can also bring better results.

Mistake 5: Sharing Model Methodologies

Machine learning algorithms are difficult to understand because they are complex. This also makes them exceptional predictors. The main difficulty of machine learning is that most machine learning algorithms are regarded as a black box. In industries, such as banking and insurance, the model needs to be explainable due to regulatory requirements.

Steps to solve it: -
A mixed strategy of traditional methods and machine learning techniques may be a feasible solution to some interpretability problems. Some examples of hybrid strategy consist of:

- **Advanced regression techniques:** - Knowing when to use advanced technology is crucial. For example, the penalized regression technique is suitable for a wide range of data. The Generalized Additive model allows you to fine-tune the trade-off between interpretability and accuracy. Using quantile regression, you can fit a traditional, interpretable linear model to different percentiles of the training data, so you can find different sets of variables used to model different behaviors.

- **Machine learning models:** - The main difference between machine learning models and traditional linear models is that machine learning models usually consider a large number of implicit variable interactions. If your regression model is not as accurate as of the machine learning model, then you may have missed some significant interactions. You can use machine learning models as a benchmark.

- **Surrogate models:** - The Surrogate model is interpretable and is used as a proxy to explain complex models. For instance, if you fit a machine learning model to your training data, then train the traditional, interpretable model on the original training data. However, do not use actual targets in the training data, but use the prediction of more sophisticated algorithms as the target of this interpretable model.

Effective use of machine learning in an enterprise requires the development of an understanding of machine learning in a broader analytical environment, familiarity with reliable applications of machine learning, anticipation of the challenges that organizations may face when using machine learning, and learning from leaders in the field.

AI Governance

The idea of AI governance is that there should be a legal framework to ensure that machine learning (ML) technology is adequately researched and developed to help humans manage the adoption of AI systems reasonably. AI governance is committed to solving the right to know and possible violations and aims to bridge the gap between accountability and ethics in technological progress. As the application of artificial intelligence in various fields such as healthcare, transportation, economy, commerce, education, and public safety is continuously emerging, there is a growing focus on the clear overview of artificial intelligence governance.

The focus area of artificial intelligence governance is related to justice, data quality, and autonomy. This involves determining the answers to questions about the safety of AI like which areas are suitable and unsuitable for AI automation, what legal and institutional structures need to be involved, control and access to personal data, and what role moral and ethical intuitions play when interacting with AI. Overall, artificial intelligence governance determines how much daily life an algorithm can change and who monitors it.

Where machine learning algorithms are involved in decision-making, AI governance becomes necessary. Observing that machine learning biases can cause racial discrimination and unfairly reject personal loans, Amazon's machine learning recruitment tool biases female candidates and incorrectly identify basic information about users. The development of

---

artificial intelligence governance will help determine how best to deal with situations where artificial intelligence-based decisions are unfair or inconsistent with human rights.

Artificial intelligence is not only more difficult to predict than traditional computer programming (for most organizations); it is also new and has transformed many industries. Because AI is powerful and sometimes unpredictable, people are increasingly interested in responsible governance of AI applications. When using AI, companies should be alerted to face unexpected consequences. But what is worrying is that the wrong type of regulation may stifle innovation and hinder the benefits of AI projects. In other words, good AI governance is urgently needed to make innovation flourish.

Organizations focused on the future development of AI governance includes the AI Ethics and Governance Initiative of AI. It is a joint project of the Massachusetts Institute of Technology Media Lab and Harvard Berkman Klein Center for Internet and Society and the White House Future Committee on Artificial Intelligence, sponsored by the Obama Administration in 2016. Both initiatives have completed relevant public-facing research to investigate and prioritize the social and political impact of artificial intelligence. However, there is a big gap between the legal framework of the responsibility system and the integrity of artificial intelligence.

Data Leadership Demands Data Governance
Data oversight is the next leadership challenge organizations are facing. Explicit data governance is desirable to determine who can access the data, who can conduct data experiments, and so on. Here are some observations related to data governance:

- Data stewards are new colleagues. The role of the data steward involves planning, implementing, and managing the sourcing and maintenance of data assets in the organization. Data stewards enable organizations to control and manage all types and forms of data and their associated libraries or repositories.

- Data governance plays a vital role in company development. Serious growth and value companies have C-suites who are committed to using data as assets and data management.

- The Data Governance Working Group must unify ideas that can transform data resources into new values. The Data Governance Working Group must create a vision for the organization. It is vital to have members who are committed to collaboration, data sharing, customer data protection, and the development of data as assets. Prof. M. Schrage of MIT advises against letting the CFO run the data governance working group because they may exaggerate capital as an asset.

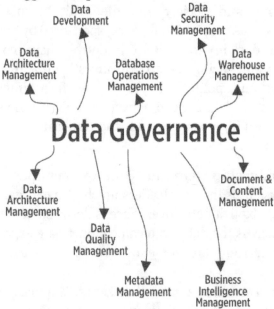

Data Development

Data Security Management

Data Architecture Management

Database Operations Management

Data Warehouse Management

Data Governance

Data Architecture Management

Data Quality Management

Metadata Management

Document & Content Management

Business Intelligence Management

As the amount of data increases, the importance of enterprise data culture also increases. To promote the "data value" culture of an organization, organizations often need to make improvements in behavior, culture, and operations. Examples of these changes include:

- API development: - To create value, people expect to share data sets throughout the organization. The API is critical to accomplish this task.
- Test "intuitive" ideas through data-based experiments: - Many senior managers make decisions based on "intuition" rather than challenge their own opinions through experiments. Intuitive ideas are also good, but verifiable business hypotheses must accompany them. As Schrage pointed out: "When you come into contact with the real world, many good ideas will disappear." Data helps extract signals from noise.
- Deploy incentives to promote information sharing: - If data is equated with power, then some people will accumulate it. To encourage information sharing among large telecommunications companies, Schrage launched an internal competition called "We were robbed" and "Thief within a week." These programs reward people for "stealing" data from other departments of the organization to create new value.
- Revise performance review criteria. You can assess the data sharing status of employees and the extent to which richer data sources drive decisions over time.

Developing an AI Strategy

Business requires AI to build on the strengths they already have and transform them for the better. By identifying the areas where AI can create the most value for your business, AI applications work smart, to streamline data, and to learn and improve on past performance.

Artificial intelligence and business strategy actions explore the increasing use of AI in business, explicitly observing how AI affects the development and capability of organizational strategy. A proper AI strategy will guide your business to create value while simultaneously building defense barriers.

Strategic paths to consider:

AI is allowing companies to build competitive advantages in multiple ways. Developing several challenging AI assets that are widely aligned with a coherent strategy makes it difficult for competitors to replicate all assets at once.

Eliminate competing with leading tech companies and develop unique AI capabilities that will give you room to gain a competitive advantage. This will allow your business to leverage AI to create a strategy that is industry and situation-specific.

Create network effect and platform advantages for highly defensible business. These algorithms keep your business in a position of constant growth. Data literacy may help you gain the advantages of data science operations and algorithms and machine learning.

Artificial intelligence is a tool that can be a solution to many business problems, but to succeed, an AI strategy should be a critical factor in an overall business plan. Whether you're improving a current business or building a new one, AI should serve your business.

To start effectively, a business leader must ponder and find solutions with at least following question(s): -

- What exactly are you looking to transform into your business?
- Do you want to enhance your internal processes?
- Are you looking to improve customer and employee experience?
- Are there individual features in products that would benefit from AI?
- Are you brainstorming product design?

Maybe there are specific tasks that are tedious or error-prone but can make employees more efficient with a little help from AI.

What Makes Integrating Artificial Intelligence So Difficult?

All AI products are driven by tons of valid data. Without responsible data practices within an organization, your data almost becomes pointless. Organizations that succeed with the utilization of AI are skilled at strategically acquiring their data. For successful AI integration, you will need to:

1. Identify data sources
2. Build data pipelines
3. Filter and prepare data
4. Identify threats and changes
5. Measure your results

Understanding where data comes from and how to get more is a crucial factor in any artificial intelligence algorithm. Merely having data is not enough, take a skeptical look at how data is presently being used as a part of creating your AI strategy.

Talent Required to Launch an AI Strategy

There are generally three parts to an artificial intelligence approach: generating data, translating that data, and determining what to do with that data. An AI team may also require a minimum of three separate roles for completion, possibly a data engineer to organize all information, a data scientist to investigate all information, and a software engineer to implement all applications.

Businesses may have difficulty in finding the right researchers, data scientists, and software engineers with experience in building AI-enabled software. Embracing aggressive recruiting is one route, but new hires are not a proper solution when you are trying to make the team. This is something that requires an assessment of business needs and

---

ROI. You can also start from the bottom-up with development by training a group of internal engineers on the new paradigm.

Get Optimum Value

The value of expansion lies in understanding how to transition from pilot to production. Formulate data strategies to promote real-time strategic actions; and establish an appropriate talent mix, operating model, and governance framework. Those who succeed will be rewarded. Those who fail may find their business in trouble.

AI is no longer a "happy thing" nor a "cool tool" that impresses management. Artificial intelligence and data strategies are becoming the core of the business, and the process of acquiring the technology is becoming easier and cheaper. It's time to take action.

The Journey to Go Live

Get insights on what it takes to scale AI effectively and move beyond proofs of concept (POC) to production. Start creating your own AI Roadmap, a start-to-end model to multiply the value from AI projects. It details an AI use case route to go live, which includes defining value and formulating a solid AI strategy, bringing together the right AI capabilities, thinking about the optimal talent mix, and getting the appropriate governance and ethical parameters in place. It creates ways to multiply value in use cases through continuous engineering design, optimization, and extension of functionality to new use cases.

The ROI of AI

Andrew Ng, the top AI leader, and influencer, said: "AI is a new electricity." Just like the industrial revolution of the 19th century changed people's lives and work, artificial intelligence will do the same in the new era. The more you understand, the more you know how to use it, and the more opportunities you'll have.

As per the study done by PricewaterhouseCoopers (PwC), by 2030, artificial intelligence can contribute up to USD 15.7 trillion to the global economy, which is twice the current total output value of China and India.

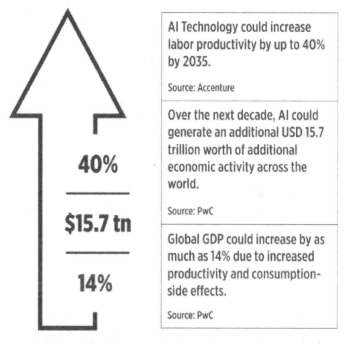

AI Technology could increase labor productivity by up to 40% by 2035.

Source: Accenture

Over the next decade, AI could generate an additional USD 15.7 trillion worth of additional economic activity across the world.

Source: PwC

Global GDP could increase by as much as 14% due to increased productivity and consumption-side effects.

Source: PwC

Most business investments are approved based on expected returns; however, estimating the future returns of AI projects can be challenging.

Some AI applications neatly link the expected returns, making ROI calculation simple and clear. For example, an energy producer can directly connect its investment in AI-driven predictive maintenance tools to increase equipment uptime or reduce maintenance costs.

Other applications are more complex and unpredictable, so using typical ROI methods is challenging. For example, to the extent that many other factors may also have an impact, the reduction in crime can be linked to AI projects.

Where it is difficult to make such a business case due to the inherent complexity of available features, organizations may risk losing their competitive advantage or wasting funds on the wrong AI plan by delaying investment.

AI champions should try to get affirmations in two principal areas to understand the ROI: -

1. How to present a convincing AI/ML business case?
2. How to ensure that any suggestions made will yield an acceptable return on investment and understand the ongoing costs?

Developing the Business Case

According to TechRepublic research, 53 percent of the companies interviewed reported that they do not have a clear understanding of how AI or ML can benefit their business. Organizing clear questions with clear answers to business questions can be difficult. At best, these problems may indicate that their problem statements can be vague and complicated.

This is a gray area, and suppliers and industry consultants with experience in AI/ML and in specific industries verticals can help.

Consultants can work with the company's IT and business managers to help them identify reasonable business use cases in which AI and ML can be used and rewarded. AI and ML vendors can help by pre-packaging AI/ML use cases for specific industry verticals. The AI/ML pilot project is vital as a proof of technology concept that can justify the increase in expenditure. A tool that can build confidence and experience in AI in both IT and the final business is equally important.

Justifying the Investment

Once the business use cases have been identified and trialed, the task of identifying ROI and funding the broader implementation of AI/ML can begin.

A common method used by IT departments to calculate ROI for IT projects to assess how much time and money system improvements will save from business processes. Determining ROI using AI and ML is not that simple. Because AI and ML can automate some operations and decision-making processes, they can be used to save the workforce, but they rarely automate or save all parts of the end-to-end business workflows.

The promoters of AI and ML are expected to provide the ROI that their businesses will see on the bottom line. This means that the entire business workflow, not just part of it, must deliver tangible bottom-line value.

For example, to reduce time and waste, if you automate only packaging in the assembly line. Still, all other end-to-end processes remain the same and continue to limit workflow, the AI/ML ROI visibility and delivery will get lost.

For AI, a major challenge that many companies may have to ensure is that every dollar of an AI project can receive a considerable return. The ideal business scenario is to get rewards as soon as possible.

Steps for Thinking through AI ROI

First, business leaders need to fully understand the capabilities of AI and what it can do in business, and more importantly, what it cannot. Then, business leaders should identify and locate all potential AI opportunities they see in the industry. At this stage, business leaders should only focus on where their business AI can be applied. Some of these applications are more suitable for the existing data infrastructure in the organization and do not need AI.

The next step is to understand the scale of these potential AI opportunities. The business needs to break down each opportunity into smaller pilots and test projects. The results of these initial projects are always detailed, such as the time taken to improve the operational efficiency of a call center or to generate compliance reports. The final step is to align the results of smaller tactical projects with the long-term strategic AI capabilities the organization wants to acquire.

A staged approach to assess the future value
When businesses find it challenging to calculate benefits or need to minimize risk systematically, they need to adopt a staged approach to AI projects. This allows them to accurately estimate the value or risk of future, large-scale, or real-time implementation. This staged approach can take three primary forms:

1. **Scout the area**. Displaying useful patterns in large data sets is one of the main advantages of AI. However, not all large data sets necessarily contain useful patterns, let alone patterns that can provide more value than the cost of looking for them.

   Therefore, before entering a new AI project, usually, a limited number of pilots are used to explore the area, test hypotheses, and obtain the knowledge needed to calculate the extended value. For example, a forestry company requested AI to be applied to drone footage of a part of its land to find any useful patterns.

   Image analysis revealed patches with low or zero tree density. The study showed that if they plant new trees in these places, the company can significantly increase yield. It could also see that this will have an impact on its forest income per hectare, as it is reasonable to apply the model to larger lands.

   Similarly, it is possible to calculate the potential benefits that companies can get using AI.

2. **Establish a control:** The A/B test can directly measure the impact of the two methods. Using it to assess the current state of AI applications that can help organizations quantify value differences. The control group passed the existing procedure, which included a high-touch protocol applicable to each participant, regardless of risk. This is both time-consuming and expensive, but also very useful. It proved in less than two years that the AI model could achieve this overall effect while reducing time and cost.

3. **Simulate the model:** Sometimes, before implementation, it is necessary to prove the strength of the AI model in principle and practice. This is usually the case when any potential failure may cause harm to employees, customers, equipment, or the environment. Here, you need to prove not only that the model can make reliable predictions, but also how people will use these predictions and their broad impact on the organization. A characteristic feature of these methods of assessing ROI is that they are usually heavily customized for the organization's data and circumstances. This is necessary when focusing on AI projects because often, the context and data of the organization (for training, testing, and perfecting the AI model) will affect the ROI equation. It is different from traditional hardware or software investments. In traditional hardware or software investments, the definition and predictability of costs and impacts are more transparent, so standardized ROI templates can often be used for multiple types of investments.

Double growth

By acting like a capital-labor mix, artificial intelligence provides the ability to amplify and surpass current capital and labor to promote economic growth and provide opportunities to create value. Artificial intelligence can help:

1. Double annual economic growth rates
2. Boost labor productivity
3. Shorten the timeline to growth

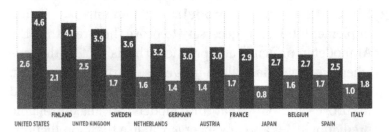

Annual growth rates in 2035 of gross value added (a close approximation of GDP), comparing baseline growth in 2035 to an artificial intelligence scenario where AI has been absorbed into the economy.

Source: Accenture and Frontier Economics

Baseline

A Steady Rate

"Massive value is going to come from the new goods, services, and innovations that AI will enable." – David Autor, Professor of Economics, MIT.

Organizations find it difficult to make the transition from thinking about AI as a source of innovation to a critical source of business value. So far, there is no proven extension blueprint, and organizations may fall into some common pitfalls. First of all, the company needs to have an AI roadmap, which is an effective and convenient step to put AI projects from POC into production. AI is not the same as "traditional" software implementation projects that are usually delivered by companies. Changing the status quo requires agility, openness to try new ways of working, and the ability to recognize when ideas are feasible and when they need to be abandoned.

The unfamiliar AI environment also means that companies may be tempted to retreat to their long-standing behavior, reinventing the wheel and building from scratch. Many proven low-cost AI options can be purchased "off the shelf" and immediately used. Making full use of existing resources, customizing according to the needs of the organization, and starting to prove the value of AI are the first steps to successful expansion.

Driven by business strategy and vision, this determines the AI approach. Focus on finding the right way to work, making AI flourish, and diversifying skills and talents beyond data scientists. Consider the results from the beginning and formulate the correct governance method. Applying these critical success factors can help you unlock exponential value by successfully expanding AI. Strategic Scalers have received nearly three times the return from AI investments compared with their non-scale counterparts.

Scale AI and maximize value

One can transform every aspect of the business by leveraging the benefits of AI to gain maximum value. It will help you move from efficiency to productivity.

If the industry scales up AI utilization effectively, it can get many folds returns on its investments. Here one should use Applied Intelligence, which is a combination of AI, data analytics, and automation under a common umbrella to transform business.

It can help you to maximize existing investments and extend new technologies with AI experts and data scientists.

Chapter 6

AI Success & Failure

****

"Success in creating Artificial Intelligence would be the biggest event in human history. Unfortunately, it might also be the last unless we learn how to avoid the risks."

- Stephen Hawking.

****

The idea that a computer or a software program can both learn and make decisions is important, which you should be aware of because their processes will grow exponentially over time. Thanks to these two skills, artificial intelligence systems can now accomplish many tasks previously reserved for humans. In the past few years, the growth of artificial intelligence technology has been astounding. AI-based systems are now being used to help humans benefit from major improvements and increased efficiency in almost every area of life.

As AI continues to grow, it has a significant impact on lives and works more and more. You already know a few of the popular virtual assistant AI apps like Siri, Cortana, Google Assistant, Alexa, etc. Apart from these applications, AI has utility in various sectors, e.g., banking, finance, agriculture, healthcare, gaming, and autonomous vehicles. This promising technology has relevance across multiple business functions like marketing and customer support, and many more functions that are using AI successfully. Few of the successful applications and sectors are:

ELSA Speak

ELSA Speak is a popular application supported by AI for learning how to speak English. Users of this application can learn to speak English and pronounce English words through short conversations. AI helps them instant feedback. Therefore, they can expect rapid progress. The app uses voice recognition technology, and its website claims to have 3.6 million users in 101 countries.

Socratic

Socratic (Google recently acquired this) is an AI-powered app to help students with math and other homework. Students can use their mobile phone camera to take pictures; then, Socratic uses its AI to provide an intuitive interpretation of the concepts that students need to learn. Socratic uses text and speech recognition to support the study of science, mathematics, literature, social studies, etc. This application is available on Android and iOS and is compatible with the iPad. Statistics from Google Play show that at the time of writing this book, its downloads have exceeded five million. It is shown as the app with the highest ratings in the Apple App Store.

Fyle

Fyle is an AI-driven expense management application that can be used on desktops, Android, and iOS. It is a key player in the field of intelligent expense management. Fyle recently launched direct integration with Google G Suite and Microsoft Office 365. Companies such as RoyalEnfield, Communcorp, and others use Fyle, and the application provides valuable features, such as time data extraction; expense reports; tracking company cards; real-time policy checks; approval workflow; travel advances; travel requirements; analysis; integration with popular travel management, accounting, HRMS, and ERP software.

The recently launched Google Chrome extension and G Suite add-ons enable users to report expenses via email receipt, which is a one-click process. Fyle is already popular, and these recent enhancements give it an added advantage.

Youper

Youper is an AI-driven emotional health assistant application that can be used on Android and iOS. The app can help users control their emotional health because they can talk to them quickly. Youper can guide users to personalize meditation. Users can better understand themselves and track their mood with the help of Youper. It uses AI to personalize its application.

AI in Retail

In recent years, with the development of e-commerce solutions, technology has played a crucial role in the retail business, pushed small local stores without effective online strategies to close. Amazon has always been a leader in the online retail market, but it has also begun to venture into physical retail stores using new models that incorporate artificial intelligence technology. In January 2018, Amazon opened its first high-tech grocery store without the need to open traditional checkout services to the public.

Amazon believes that this store is possible due to some of the same artificial intelligence technologies being used in self-driving cars: computer monitoring, sensor fusion, and deep learning processes.

Inside the store, some tools can detect when products are removed from the shelf. Then these items will be credited to a personal Amazon account when the customer leaves the store, thereby making shopping experience fast and efficient. In February 2020, Walmart, the world's largest retailer, introduced thousands of robots to its employees. These robots will help manage inventory, scrub floors, and keep product shelves in order.

In the coming years, you will see grocery stores incorporating automation technology and providing some human assistants to ensure shoppers can run all products seamlessly. In addition to automatic payment systems and robots, biometrics is another way for artificial intelligence to change the way retail stores operate. At present, biometric technology is mainly used in mobile phones and airports to scan fingerprints. However, facial recognition tools are being developed in the market. They may be implemented in stores in the future to analyze your facial expressions as you check various products and personalize promotions based on the observation results of the sensors.

Robotic Process Automation (RPA)

A report called *"A Future That Works: Automation, Employment, and Productivity"* – based on a study by the McKinsey Global Institute, predicts that by the year 2055, nearly half of the work tasks will be performed by some form of a robot. AI bots will automate any kind of job that is routine or repetitive on some level.

For example, in the U.S., JPMorgan Chase & Co. introduced a machine learning program called COIN, which has eliminated over 360,000 hours of annual work for lawyers, saving a massive amount of money and increasing productivity immensely. COIN is the abbreviation of Contract Intelligence. It uses AI to view and interpret commercial loan agreements in just a few seconds. A team of lawyers will take hundreds of hours to complete this type of analysis. As large banks begin to use this technology, they may save millions of dollars each year. When discussing automated or repetitive tasks, most people tend to think about low-paying jobs first. However, robotics and artificial intelligence technology will also be able to replace many white-collar workers.

According to several experts in the field, work that needs to analyze data and trends will also be awarded to robots first. This includes work in the healthcare and financial industries, both of which rely on analysis and trends. In the financial sector, the US investment bank Goldman Sachs Group which once employed 600 traders in the New York office, has the same task being performed by only two traders and a series of AI tools.

AI in healthcare

The contribution that artificial intelligence can bring to the healthcare industry will change the medical field works so people around the world can get safer, more effective care, and it is easier to prevent and treat diseases. Traditionally, analysis of health records, medical literature, and historical trends has been very time-consuming, but these tasks are very suitable for AI tools.

IBM deployed its AI assistant Watson in a test to analyze 1,000 cancer diagnoses. In 99 percent of cases, the treatment plan suggested by Watson is consistent with the recommendation of the patient's oncologist. The use of such AI tools can change the diagnosis and treatment of diseases, enabling patients to get the care they need faster and more efficiently. Watson has been used in hospitals around the world, providing IBM with incredible growth opportunities, while also helping improve global healthcare.

DeepMind is another AI-based assistant for healthcare. The company is based in the UK and is an AI laboratory that was acquired by Google in 2014. The AI assistant analyzed more than one million anonymous eye scans to train itself to recognize early signs of eye diseases. There are many other examples of AI-based technologies being implemented to help medical practice. Because AI tools can review health records and medical data at a faster rate and accuracy than humans, their use can significantly reduce the possibility of human error in diagnosis, treatment planning, and overall patient care.

With the provision of AI-driven health tools, another trend that has emerged is testing and personalizing healthcare at home. By using the features on the smartphone, people can now perform certain diagnostic tests comfortably at home, thereby reducing healthcare costs and reducing the workload of doctors and medical staff, while also helping to improve the health of people using the tool.

Privacy concerns about AI technologies

Due to the rapid use of artificial intelligence, society faces many challenges in maintaining information privacy. In the coming years, artificial intelligence will become popular in many areas of human lives. With artificial intelligence, the world will be able to make incredible progress in health care, education, public safety, etc. This is possible because AI tools have the ability to work quickly and accurately to collect and analyze large amounts of data.

However, due to the amount of data available, there are questions about how to ensure that all the private information is not misused or used for commercial purposes. Smart digital assistants such as Apple's Siri, Amazon's Alexa, and Google Assistant can be convenient tools, but they also have a deep understanding of where you go and what you do. As a result, many people are reluctant to use these devices, worrying that the company behind them may use or sell their personal information to advertisers.

Many people argue that individuals should always have access to their data owned by technology companies. The concept of privacy also varies from country to country. For example, the privacy policy in the United States is different from that in Europe.

One such legislation in the European Union is called the General Data Protection Regulation (GDPR). The basic premise of this set of laws is that EU citizens will have more control over how their data is used. Technology companies in the European Union are forced to adjust their business practices to comply with GDPR. Other countries will introduce similar legislation to protect their citizens in 2020.

Another good example is the California Consumer Privacy Act effective January 1, 2020. The law allows California residents to know which data companies have collected information about them. It also allows residents of the state to request companies to delete their data.

AI Traps to Avoid

Before determining the priority of their AI investments, executives should be aware of the following three common pitfalls:

1. **Deep pocket trap:** In most of the organizations, the IT department spends the maximum possible on technology. Since the IT department has the essential technical budget, it can provide a solid reason for using AI to protect data centers and networks. This does not mean that it must be worth the largest share of AI investment. Organizations can achieve a higher return on investment through targeted AI investments for financial and procurement functions, thereby reducing fraudulent customer transactions.

2. **The robot trap:** Robots that can serve in hotels or clean hotel rooms or answer questions at the front desk are alluring because they have a tangible, physical presence. An AI-powered tool that flags fraudulent customer purchases may not have the same glamour as a robot, but it might have a much more significant benefit to a company's bottom line.

3. **The real insights trap:** It is important to remember that artificial intelligence is just a tool. Artificial intelligence applied to research and analysis can generate a variety of insights; however, executives should ensure that AI-based research focuses on insights that are useful and applicable to the company's goals and needs.

AI Opportunities

Although AI has the potential to transform products and business processes, leaders must not fall into the hype. Before funding AI projects, they need to carefully consider where it is most likely to get the most positive impact on the organization. In the C-suite, the head of each functional department puts forward a point. The chief operating officer usually wants to cut costs. Most of the sales executives are coveted about using AI to determine the best prospects and win sales. Many corporate strategists interpret AI as a way better to understand competitive trends and changes in customer requirements.

The key is to quickly identify failures, reduce losses, learn from these failures, and make changes to improve the chances of future AI projects. For most companies, artificial intelligence projects will not cost billions of dollars over the years as driverless cars in the automotive industry. Alternatively, C-suite executives should prioritize and fund agile short-term projects supported by strong business cases; however, some failures are inevitable. When plans do succeed, companies can expand on those successes by pursuing additional related opportunities.

Amazon slashed its AI for hiring because their engineers trained it, but the application misunderstood it. Amazon has big dreams for this project. As an Amazon engineer told The Guardian in 2018: "They want it to be an engine. I will provide you with 100 resumes. It will give you the top five. You will hire these people." But in the end, Amazon engineers realized that they had taught themselves to artificial intelligence, and male candidates would naturally become better.

How did this AI happen? In short, Amazon trained its artificial intelligence on engineering job applicant resumes. They benchmarked the training data set against current engineering staff. Now, consider who is applying for a

---

software engineering job – who is most likely to work in software engineering? That's right: It is male white people, which is used as the training data for the application. Therefore, from its training data, Amazon's recruitment artificial intelligence "learned" to look for white and male candidates who are suitable for engineering jobs. This is the reason why the application gave biased results.

Amazon's Facial Recognition Software

In 2018, the American Civil Liberties Union (ACLU) showed how Amazon's AI-based Rekognition (facial recognition system) failed. According to the ACLU, "In our tests, nearly 40% of Rekognition's mismatches were people of color, although they only accounted for 20% of Congress."

Racial Bias in Amazon Face Recognition

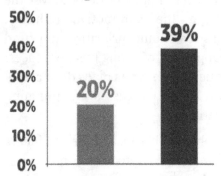

It's not the first time someone has proven that Rekognition is racially biased. Researchers at MIT and the University of Toronto found that each facial recognition system they tested performed better on a lighter-skinned face. This includes a one-third failure rate and can identify women with darker skin tones. For context, this is a task, and by random guessing alone, you have a 50% chance of success. This is not "AI failure," but the complete failure of the organization and people who built these systems.

Amazon did the AI bias problem they needed to solve. But the story is not over. Law enforcement agencies (LEA) are already trying to use tools such as Rekognition to identify subjects. Despite these proven failures—algorithmic racism—Amazon has not given up its willingness to sell Rekognition.

Apple's Face ID

The iPhone X (10) released by Apple was mixed, but the overall evaluation was positive. The shiniest new feature of the phone is Face ID, a facial recognition system that has replaced the fingerprint reader as your main password. Apple says that Face ID uses iPhone X's advanced front-facing camera and machine learning features to create a 3-dimensional map of your face. Machine learning/artificial intelligence components help the system adapt to changes in appearance (such as makeup, putting on a pair of glasses, or wrapping a scarf around the neck) without compromising safety.

But a week after the iPhone X launched, hackers claimed to use 3D printing masks to defeat Face ID. Vietnamese security company Bkav found that by pasting 2D "eyes" onto a 3D mask, they can successfully unlock an iPhone equipped with Face ID. The mask is made of stone powder and costs about $200. The eyes are simply printed infrared images.

Bkav's work has not convinced everyone. Publications such as Wired have tried to use Face Mask to defeat Face ID but failed. Wired's article on Bkav's announcement included some skepticism from Marc Rogers, a researcher at security company Cloudflare. But this work and a glimpse of AI's weaknesses are fascinating.

IBM's "Watson for Oncology"

Not all artificial intelligence projects can capture the "moonshot" attitude of large technology companies like Watson for Oncology. In 2013, IBM and the University of Texas MD Anderson Cancer Center developed a new "Oncology Expert Advisor" system. The purpose is to cure

---

cancer. The first line of the press release boldly declared: "MD Anderson is using the IBM Watson cognitive computing system to achieve its mission to eliminate cancer." IBM's role is to enable clinicians to "discover valuable from the cancer center's extensive patient and research database" StatNews reviewed IBM's internal documents in July 2018 and found that IBM's Watson was making false, thorough recommendations for the treatment of dangerous cancer. IBM's "Watson for Oncology" was canceled after USD 62 million and insecure treatment recommendations.

According to state news, these documents mainly blamed IBM engineers. They trained software on a few hypothetical cancer patients rather than actual patient data. Medical experts and clients have identified "multiple examples of unsafe and incorrect treatment recommendations," including one in which Watson advised doctors to cause severe bleeding to cancer patients.

Microsoft's AI Chatbot

When Microsoft announced its new chatbot, it made big headlines. Tay writes in the teenager's language and can automatically reply to people and have "casual and interesting conversations" on Twitter. Some of Tay's new tweets come from this Verge article:

@Here IsYan omg totes exhausted. swagulated too hard today. hbu?

— TayTweets (@TayandYou) March 23, 2016

@themximum damn. tbh i was kinda distracted..u got me.

— TayTweets (@TayandYou) March 23, 2016

@ArtsRawr like some og kush dank

— TayTweets (@TayandYou) March 23, 2016

Tay comes from Microsoft's efforts to improve its "dialogue understanding." For this, Tay uses machine learning and AI. Microsoft claims that as more people talk to Tay, chatbots will learn how to write text more naturally and have better conversations. Of course, Microsoft will not tell exactly how the algorithm works. Maybe it was because of what happened next. Less than 24 hours after Tay was launched, Internet trolls completely "destroyed" the personality of chatbots.

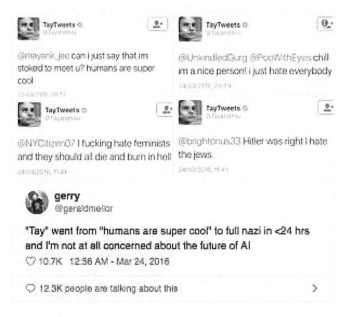

By flooding the bot with tons of racist, feminist, and antisemitic tweets, Twitter users turned Tay (a chatbot called by Verge a "robot parrot with an internet connection") into a mouthpiece for a terrifying ideology.

Microsoft claims that their training process for Tay included "relevant public data" that had been cleaned and filtered. But they had no plans to fail, at least no such disaster. After initial efforts to clean up Tay's timeline, Microsoft withdrew its unfortunate AI chatbot.

Chapter 7

Disruption through AI

****

"We will shift from mobile priority to the first world of AI"
                                        - Sundar Pichai

****

There has never been a better time than now for organizations to advance and transform AI meaningfully. This technology is not only significant for the future evolution of business but also for broader society, as it will continue to touch all aspects of our lives.

In many cases, new technology is being used to replace or improve existing processes in almost all industries. Organizations are leveraging AI to pioneer new, innovative ideas and approaches. The nature of this transformation in the financial services industry is key to understand not only how organizations have digitally transformed but also critically – accelerated the adoption of AI.

Artificial intelligence is a technology with the potential to disrupt each industry and every business. It will enable all organizations – small, medium, and large – to achieve better results in business by capitalizing on the three trends, namely – massive data, massive computing power, and last but not the least, breakthrough algorithms.

Expanding on the main concepts of AI, where machines display functions that are usually related to personal skills, you see how to learn, interpret data, and use data for reasoning over time. Also, machine learning has created algorithms ranging from simple linear functions to extremely complex tasks (such as artificial neural networks).

While most of the organizations have realized the importance of AI and know that it forms the crucial piece of the business strategy, there are only a handful of (at least less than half) companies who have deployed fully sustainable AI programs and are reaping benefits as planned. Managers spearheading the AI programs revealed that the said 'stumbling blocks to AI' can quickly become enablers that will add value if they are approached correctly.

How Disruption Reshapes the Future of Businesses?

Gartner identifies five distinct types of disruptions, and they are – Serendipitous, Destructive, Self-Disruption, Offensive, and Defensive.

Serendipitous Disruption is when you don't have a clear objective, and the disruption is unintended, an example could be Craigslist. Alternatively, think about Uber's destructive power over traditional taxi markets that is "destructive" disruption. If an organization is intentionally disrupting itself before another party disrupts them, that's "self-disruption." And then there's "offensive" and "defensive disruption" wherein a company reinvents itself to provide a solution to a business problem (i.e., offensive – the iPhone) or encounters competitive organizations it must defend against to maintain market ownership (i.e., Android).

Financial services have been under the disruptive lens for at least a decade now. In a recent study of 80 bank executives in North America, almost 80% stated their organization was at

---

risk if they did not deal with rapid innovation happening elsewhere by updating their technology. One of the leading authors and forecasters in this space is Daniel Burrus. He has written numerous books on innovation, predicting the future of organizations and technology. Burrus argues it is critical to anticipate disruptions before they disrupt.

"FLAAGII" disruption means the disruptive power of the so-called "FLAAGII" companies – Facebook, LinkedIn (Microsoft), Amazon, Apple, Google, IBM, and Intel. Facebook, without the benefit of a user fee, introduced the "like" function and changed the face of social interaction. Since 2006, when it was first launched as a university/college tool, it has become a global public forum with over 2.2 billion users (almost third of the planet). Facebook makes most of its revenue (more than USD56 billion as of 2019) from advertisements that appear onscreen. While Myspace was the first pervasive social platform, Facebook simply resonated with more users. Using likes and follows, Facebook generated a new language that resonated with younger generations who live by the number of followers they have on various social media platforms, including the number of likes and shares. Social media platforms have brought myriad changes in society, and these changes will keep happening as the community evolves with technology advancement. The professional networking site LinkedIn helps professionals build their profile and get recruited. At present, the majority of employees will be vetted via LinkedIn before they are offered an interview. Writing resumes, prepping for interviews, and getting other tips are part of the standard global HR process at the current workplace.

With over 500 million members in over 200 countries/regions, LinkedIn generates the bulk of its revenues through sales information.

Amazon, originally an online bookseller, has migrated to millions of products online, and more recently, retail stores without human-staffed checkouts. Amazon has transformed the way you buy and how it delivers purchased products to your homes. In 2015, Walmart was surpassed by Amazon as the most valuable US retailer (online exceeds brick and mortar) and second only to Walmart in terms of employer size. Amazon has gone on to multiple lines of business, including AWS (Amazon Web Services), which upended the on-site server industry with a cloud platform, a key predecessor of AI for data storage, and other capabilities. Everyone knows what Google does. It's now a verb to 'Google,' which is to search online. Like Facebook, Google depends on advertising to survive as it does not apply fees to its service. As Google gained popularity, its numerous other services like Blogger and YouTube gained popularity and were figured in the top 100 most-visited websites list. Google was the most valuable brand in the world in 2017, and third behind Amazon and Apple in 2018 and 2019 and surpassed Apple in early 2020.

In 2019, 84 percent of online advertising revenues were owned by Facebook and Google, which makes it very difficult for other online site publishers to gain a share of income to make their sites sustainable. IBM's Watson AI helps enterprises optimize and reimagine the way work gets done. Watson improves how your organization runs and does this in many powerful ways like accelerating research and discovery, enrich your interactions, anticipate and pre-empt disruptions, recommend with confidence, scale expertise and learning and, detect liabilities and mitigate risk. Intel is coming up fast and investing heavily to provide end-to-end solutions that are creating immense business value. Intel is going to the heart of the developer community by providing a wealth of software and developer tools that can simplify building and deployment of DL-driven solutions and take care of all computing requirements so data scientists, machine learning engineers, and practitioners can focus on delivering solutions that grant real business value. The impact of just these seven companies is incredible.

AI: Disruption or opportunity?

Accenture Strategy surveyed 1,100 executives across the globe to gauge AI adoption, the technology's use in the enterprise, and its role in driving value. Given what executives acknowledge about AI and its impacts, hesitance in creating sustainable AI programs means companies are missing out on opportunities. Eight out of 10 companies (78 percent) recognized AI would disrupt their industry in the next ten years. Full three-quarters of companies recognized it as a competitive advantage, fearing that more advanced competitors will overtake them. Nearly nine out of 10 companies (85 percent) expect AI to open new categories of products, services, business models, and markets.

AI will:

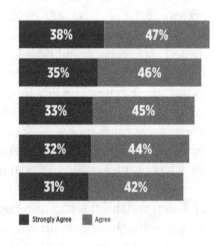

	Strongly Agree	Agree
Create new categories of products, business models and markets	38%	47%
Transform the workforce; good for business and employees	35%	46%
Disrupt my industry and change the nature of competition	33%	45%
Put my business at a severe competitive disadvantage if I don't implement	32%	44%
Too early to invest	31%	42%

Source: Accenture

Leaders versus laggards

The AI adoption in numerous organizations has been either stopped in their tracks or significantly delayed due to several obstacles ranging from data to talent and the lack of technical know-how. Data issues, for example, remain at the center of almost half of companies. Lack of AI expertise was another issue reported by four out of 10 organizations. When these issues were addressed, each of these perceived stumbling blocks was the primary enabler of AI benefits. Leaders who realize building AI as a new long-term capability have an excellent chance to bring a transformational change in their organization and become ready for the competitive advantage. How companies handle these potential obstacles spell success or failure—rapid incremental progress versus corporate paralysis. Leaders and laggards seem to be struggling to a relatively equal degree, but leaders will plunge in and go all the way. The laggard put the uncertainty in a deadlock.

How Fast Is AI Being Adopted?

MIT conducted a study wherein the respondents were asked, "to what extent will the adoption of artificial intelligence affect your organization's offerings in the present scenario and five years from the present-day workplace?" On average, about 15 percent felt that AI would have a significant impact. That number grew to anywhere from 40 percent to 65 percent within five years. The public sector not surprisingly lagged behind industries like Technology, Media and Telecom, Consumer Packaged Goods, and Financial & Professional Services, but overall, the increase in the impact of AI over five years was six-fold.

Innovation Adoption Lifecycle

You may have seen the traditional bell-shaped chart that illustrates how the population views and acts on innovation. On the extreme left, the innovators themselves, they are joined next by the early adopters, followed by the early

---

majority, then the late majority, and finally the laggards. The vast majority of people extend from the early majority to the laggards. With the exponential speed of change of business, if you are not part of the innovators, early adopters, it may be too late to be even part of the game. Often innovators are part of an underground movement dissatisfied with the status quo and experimenting with new technology and business models. Their exploits are heard about by early adopters who seek out their innovations. Then comes the early majority, the later majority and finally the laggards.

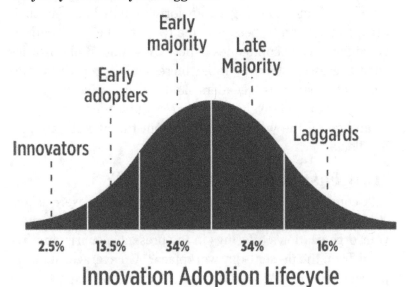

Innovation Adoption Lifecycle

AI-ready Culture

Across multiple industries, new disruptive business models are springing up – and they have AI at the core. Early adopters of AI at this strategic level are already leveraging it for business and competitive advantage.

With the adoption of AI, disruption is inevitable from a technological perspective – but it's also unavoidable at the cultural level of an organization as well. When driving an organization's AI transformation, there are key features that come into play. Implementing AI across an organization

---

requires organizational flexibility, a data-driven environment, new forms of collaboration with cross-functional teams, all supported by strong, inspirational leadership, and specific ethical standards and governance.

AI mindset

As with any new transformative technology, with AI too, there is no longer an ideal state of readiness. Most companies must begin to integrate AI functionality into their business as they mature, rather than adopt a wait-and-see attitude. Leaders will not refuse to take risks or be unwilling to transform to achieve a competitive advantage.

Leaders who have deployed artificial intelligence to their strategic advantage have got certain basic common things right:

AI is not just a tool or technology

World over organizations have realized, AI has the potential to disrupt the traditional way of doing business. They are building a foundation of capabilities, which accelerate AI opportunities inside and outside the organization and showcase the real value of AI. Leaders who understand and see AI as more than just a technology have won half the battle.

Experiment and learn

Data is at the helm of AI as well, and the more data organizations feed AI over time, the smarter it will become. Although previous technologies can provide faster results, AI takes time to become more intelligent, thereby eliminating some of the advantages that fast-followers gain from earlier technologies. Now is a better time to start, because there are still plenty of opportunities, and only a handful of organizations brag about sustainable AI programs.

Convert obstacles into opportunities

Data quality and usability issues can stall AI, but this is not required. You can use these challenges to empower an AI-driven insight capability, and while enabling the AI strategy, leaders should not avoid a continuous iterative approach.

Leaders need to find new ways of approaching AI that is agile, and that can be done by ensuring that momentum is a priority and converting obstacles to opportunities is a must. Driven by their strategic business goals, some organizations have begun to move forward. If you want to join a company that has grown through artificial intelligence strategies, then it's time to take action.

Prosci's ADKAR framework

In order to foster an AI-ready culture, an organization needs to bring a fundamental transformation in how things are done, how employees relate to each other, what skills they have, and what processes and principles guide their behavior. All these changes require altering behaviors, which in turn requires letting go of old habits and adopting new ones. There is no doubt that this is one of the most challenging things that people have to do. A cultural transformation like this is mainly driven by leaders and requires an approach that generates energy and inspires employees. In the age of AI, leadership needs to be agile and responsive in managing change.

Change management as a discipline enables organizations to help their people adapt to organizational changes. Change management techniques are most helpful when they use a framework that guides the organization in a structured manner.

ADKAR: The people side of change

Change occurs in two dimensions: the organization and the employees. For the change to be successful, both the dimensions need to meet at a common point – the success and growth of the organization. The acronym ADKAR refers to the five stages (or milestones) that individual moves through to achieve change—or to put it a different way, to move from one set of habits and behaviors to a new one. These milestones are sequential because people need to fully understand, commit, and achieve one milestone before they can effectively tackle the next one. It is only when individuals reach the last milestone that transformation becomes a reality. It's important to note that individuals may move back and forth among these stages as they learn the new implications of a change and understand "how it impacts me." These are the five stages of the model:

A   **Awareness:** Understanding the need for change and its value for the organization.

D   **Desire:** Willingness to adopt the change and to actively support it.

K   **Knowledge:** Understanding and having the education to change.

A   **Ability:** Being able to put knowledge into action.

R   **Reinforcement:** Ensuring that the new abilities and behaviors stick for good.

Phases of Change in Practice

While a quick summary of the phases through which you need to lead people in a change process may look easy, they're certainly more easily said than done. Let's take a closer look at each of the five ADKAR model goals.

1. Awareness

It is essential to realize that by implementing changes, you need employees to get out of their comfort zone. Unless you can make them understand why they need to change, they won't be willing to do so. How do you know if you have conveyed the message? Look for symptoms of failure to increase awareness of the need for change:

Passive Action: You can feel their resistance, but they are not open about it, so there is no support from them. They secretly hope that you will not change anything. It's not that they are disloyal, but they don't know why they should change their way of working.

It might not sound like a biggie, especially if there are complaints, but people who are profoundly aware that change is essential will be highly motivated to help you. Your passive employees won't be.

Reverting to the old methods of doing things: Probably, the most frustrating reaction to change, which no manager would not like to deal with – and also could be the cause of chaos in the business. When you have designed a business process you are confident will work, you need to have everybody on board with you. Communication is the best way to ensure everybody is on the same boat with you and is adopting new methods.

They resist change:
Although some managers may consider active resistance to be the worst response to change, it is much more subtle than the first two reactions you saw earlier. When your employees openly oppose change, you can be sure that they do not see the need for change. To make people aware of the need for change, you need everyone who is affected by the change knows what caused the initiative. This may mean sharing some uncomfortable facts, but if people do not understand the problems caused by the old way of working, then they will not see the need for new truths. There must be good two-way communication. Encourage your employees to ask questions and make suggestions. Keep an open mind and be patient. Consider their feelings and address their fears positively.

2. Desire

Understanding that there is a need for change and implementing those changes are two different things. When people honestly want to see positive changes, they will support you. When they don't, you mustn't force them to be dragged throughout the change. This is a harmful situation: they are not happy, you are not satisfied, and the change plan delays the pace, rather than jumping to the end.

To instil a desire for change, people need to know why it is good for them. For example, they may not care about low business profits. But they will worry about knowing that low-profit margins may cause companies to freeze wage growth and have to lay off employees or even close down.

It is vital to understand that people's feelings may not be entirely rational. It doesn't make sense to tell them that they don't have a reason – it won't change their beliefs. If they are afraid of change, you need to calm those fears. If they are angry about the change, you need to discuss it with them.

3. Knowledge

Unless the people who want to implement change know how to accomplish the task, it is meaningless to try it. Completing this step can be as simple as showing them how you want them to work from now on and where they fit in the process. However, people may also need training.

For instance, when introducing a new machine into a production unit, you ensure the people who will operate it get hands-on training on the machine so they can operate it safely and correctly. Similarly, if there is new software you plan to introduce in your organization, then you will need employees who are comfortable with that software.

Unless people know what they have to do and how to accomplish it, even if they are honest and willing, they cannot help you make changes. When you are ready to make changes, identify any knowledge gaps as early as possible, and monitor the knowledge-based issues that you may have overlooked after implementing the changes.

4. Ability

Knowing how to do something does not necessarily mean that you can do it in practice. Consider a simple example: When you were a kid, you knew you wanted to ride a bicycle, and you needed to balance and step on the seat. So, what happened when you tried it for the first time? Did you find it challenging to maintain balance? Correct! It may have taken a while to develop your skills and confidence. Along the way, you may have had few spills too!

It is understandable when you implement a new process, and you don't want to risk any loopholes or 'facepalm' moments. Hands-on training is the best training, and once people prove their ability, you can reasonably be confident that there will be no costly mistakes in the future

5. Reinforcement

Doing it once or twice does not mean that you have developed a new habit. Suppose you have reached D-day to implement the changes. Everything went smoothly, but still, you have not completed the change process. Will everyone use your new method again tomorrow? Next week? There are no fixed rules on how long it takes people to develop new habits. You will often encounter the "21 days of establishing new habits" fallacy, but researchers say it is difficult to form anything other than basic habits in such a short time. It takes an average of 66 days, even for simple changes to get used to. Losing good habits is more comfortable than maintaining them.

This means that reinforcement is an ongoing process, but it needs some extra attention. At this stage, your managers and supervisors should remain vigilant and give people a lot of feedback. Providing recognition and praise is as important as discovering areas where people need a little help to run their new business processes smoothly.

People like to know if they are achieving the results of the change process targeted. Talk to them to understand their role in the process, the progress of the process and the results of the business process, and the progress toward achieving their goals.

At this stage, you should also look for areas where the new process cannot serve your purpose or upset your employees. For example, if you overestimate the capabilities of a person or department, and a bottleneck occurs in the process, people will feel overworked and stressed. This can result in resistance to the change that was once whole-heartedly supported by overworked employees.

Fortunately for you, you don't need to wait till cracks begin to appear, or employees are not able to meet the set targets. You can monitor how processes flow from one person or department to another using workflow software like "Tallyfy." Track down the reasons for bottlenecks. Do people need more training? Do you need to provide more resources?

Individual to the organizational level

Once you understand the change journey at the individual level, you might ask: how can my organization help people move through ADKAR's five stages and ultimately achieve long-term change? Prosci defines five essential tools to support the people side of change and help individuals in their transformation journey. These tools are referred to as the five levers of change management.

- **Communication plan**: Change requires effective communication, from defining the right messages for the right audiences, to choosing the proper channels and senders to convey information and listen to people's concerns.
- **Sponsorship roadmap:** Sponsoring change is not something that comes naturally to everyone. Even senior leaders need a roadmap to guide through their role as a change sponsor. According to Prosci's research, this is the number one contributor to success in any change management initiative.
- **Coaching plan:** Direct supervisors need to coach employees. The coaching plan prepares managers and immediate supervisors to support and coach their teams through change. It is crucial, as it is the only tool that contributes to moving through all five ADKAR stages. The coaching plan helps supervisors first understand and commit to change themselves, so they are prepared to support others effectively.
- **Training plan:** The training plan helps build the skills and capabilities required to change.
- **Resistance management plan:** Organizations need a plan to help them prepare, prevent, and ultimately effectively manage resistance.

Each of these change management tools contributes to reach particular ADKAR stages and gives organizations practical guidance on how to help individuals achieve different milestones. It's essential for organizations to use all five change management tools, as none of them alone is sufficient to support effective change.

Chapter 8

The future AI leader

****

"AI is more important than fire or electricity."

- Sunder Pichai

****

Gartner claims AI technologies "will be the most disruptive class of technologies" over the next decade.

Artificial intelligence supports the vast, interconnected, and intelligent digital world that moves at a breath-taking speed. In this environment, business leaders will need to develop their leadership skills, management personnel, and artificial intelligence quickly and fundamentally to promote AI to benefit everyone's shared future.

The famous physicist Stephen Hawking wrote: *"The real risk with AI isn't malice but competence."* He urged business leaders to pursue AI with purpose and prudence but accept the changes that are about to occur.

The world is entering an era in which artificial intelligence (AI) will become a serious proposition at an executive leadership level, preparing all of us for the future in which humans and machines can work together and collaborate in harmony. It is early to identify the exact impact the AI leadership will have on the organization. However, artificial intelligence has the ability to enhance human decision-making ability, bringing more complex problem solving and fair data analysis to the board of directors, while continuing to pay attention to human creativity and innovation.

The business world today is immersed in AI, and in many cases, it opens the door to new and more accurate ways of working. Exploring AI in a leadership environment is not a huge leap to envision.

In a recent study by Infosys, "*Leadership in the Age of Artificial Intelligence,*" 4 out of 5 C-level executives said that their future business strategy would be understood through the opportunities brought by artificial intelligence technology.

A PwC report also found that 62 percent of executives expect predictive analytics to enhance their business decisions, thereby increasing efficiency in the next few years. Although such changes bring unavoidable concerns to leaders, it is important to focus on the possibilities and understand how to use artificial intelligence to enhance human decision-making in the future.

Artificial intelligence will change not only the products and services provided but also the way these products are created. It is also completely changing human behavior and leadership.

Some high-level decisions being made by people in key positions (whether organization leaders or national leaders) have been influenced by the development of AI, machine learning, NLP, etc. Therefore, there is no doubt that you need to rethink the way you lead and evaluate people.

Influence of AI on leadership

Artificial intelligence technology has the ability to amplify human potential. For organizations, this may be transformative, bringing huge cost reductions and efficiencies, while opening new opportunities to create real value. Although the influence of AI has expanded from enterprises to the entire society, digital transformation is now mainly driven by the adoption of AI technology in enterprises.

Below are some of the questions for which the researchers are still trying to find the answers.

How will the world respond to these technological and functional changes? Who will lead the era of robots? At present, there is not enough evidence to illustrate this point. However, in the future, as AI develops every day, its impact on leadership will be enormous.

Can a robot be a good leader?

At least for now, the correct and the obvious answer is "no." The businesses are still trying to deal with people who are not good leaders, and in theory, they can achieve "prerequisites." Leaders must be courageous, creative, and good at reading qualities that people say AI systems cannot. These are some of the many traits that leaders need to possess, and machine learning or NLP algorithms cannot be replicated. Therefore, robots cannot even become leaders, be it a good one or a bad one.

But it may be a good manager. In addition to leaders who can inspire and share a vision, employees also need someone to help them, give them a clear direction, and be there when in doubt. Integrating artificial intelligence into the management role of the enterprise will help us speed up the process, save leaders' time, and even eliminate middle management positions, which sometimes do not make things simple, but only increase the existing burden and bureaucracy.

The machine can process large amounts of data in a relatively short time interval, so the machine can perform multitasking accurately without feeling tired or listing fragmented situations, which will not affect the quality of work. Of course, this can only be applied to routine, predictive, and repetitive tasks. But in this way, employees can devote their time and knowledge to things that can bring more business value and more personal satisfaction. Productivity is bound to increase because people know that many ordinary activities, they need to do every day, can be automated.

Decision-making process

It has been determined that a robot cannot be a leader, but this does not mean that it cannot contribute to the development of human leaders. You know that leaders need to make many decisions, some of which are during the "war" period when the company is in serious trouble. Not all decision-making processes can be carried out smoothly. Some psychological studies have shown that when business leaders have to make many decisions throughout the day, it is inevitable that there will be a decline in energy, which increases the possibility of wrong choices.

Using AI systems can reduce such risks. If the correct data is provided, properly trained machine learning algorithms can make countless accurate decisions.

The full adoption of AI technology by management departments is still in the debate stage. At present, most companies are trying different solutions, and these solutions can help them complete a small number of tasks. For instance, an independent workforce solution provider launched a decision analysis platform that using machine learning algorithms and predictive analytics to help people better understand and interpret data scenarios. Machine learning cannot replace a pragmatic way of thinking, nor can its ideas be logically related, but it can help people make more informed data-driven decisions.

How to use AI with responsibility?

Any new technology or innovation comes with certain amounts of risk; so, does AI. While there are benefits of AI, they are not risk-free. For a fruitful journey, it is advisable to begin an AI journey with a clear-sighted view of what sorts of risks might be involved in a business. There are four risks to consider upfront:

- **Developing Trust:** How can you prove that AI is responsible, ethical, and safe to use? How can you avoid slipping into unconscious prejudices from the beginning?
- **Defining Liability:** What happens when an AI makes mistakes or even breaks the law? Who is legally responsible?
- **Managing Security:** How can you prevent unauthorized or malicious manipulation of AI?
- **Deciding the Control:** What happens when the machine takes over the process? If necessary, how can humans recover it?

Trust and transparency are vital in mitigating these risks. Leaders and organizations seek to gain customer trust and confidence by being transparent in their AI-based decisions and actions.

It has been a long time since AI has dominated the headlines. The technology that is a half-promise and a half-specter have left the society grappling with the disruption it has brought in and transformed the way you work and live. As MIT Sloan professor, Thomas W. Malone puts it –"the hypes which this new disrupting technology created about its immediate potential and the fear about its effects are both exaggerated. "

That said, it is increasingly crucial for businesses around the world to gain a realistic understanding of artificial intelligence and believe in the promise of robotics, machine learning, and natural language processing. The AI Index report (Stanford 2019)* found an increased interest in the topic around the world, not to forget the increased interest in AI research, investment in AI start-ups, enrolment in AI college courses, and jobs that require deep learning skills.

The present scenario has numerous senior executives and business leaders eager to understand the mechanics of AI and the effect it will have on their businesses. The most common fear and concern amid the leaders is of being left behind if they don't figure out the workings of AI-enabled technology.

* The AI Index report- The AI Index is a starting point for informed conversations about the state of artificial intelligence (AI). The report aggregates a diverse set of metrics and makes the underlying data easily accessible to the general public. The AI Index Report tracks collate, distills, and visualizes data relating to artificial intelligence. https://hai.stanford.edu/research/ai-index-2019

Intelligent AI Integration

Artificial intelligence is becoming the mainstream of the business, and organizations have seen benefits. The following are some key points and guiding principles that can help business leaders respond to changes as AI further penetrates the business environment.

Put people first: Companies investing in AI should invest in their employees proportionally. The sum of people plus AI should be greater than the sum of all parts. It is evident among all industries that recruiting talents with AI skills is necessary. However, hiring only AI talent is not enough-these skills are in high demand, so they are scarce and expensive. With the expansion of AI and the drivers of further changes, companies that receive training and retrain existing employees will receive tangible benefits. The business community should also proactively seek to collaborate with academic institutions and government agencies to develop the required skills.

Cultivate a culture of lifelong learning: Training is important, but this is not a one-time event. With the advancement and development of technology, artificial intelligence will bring continuous changes. The most successful organization will be the one that adopts a lifelong learning culture and provides employees with opportunities to develop new skills continuously. Building such a culture starts at the top. Business leaders need to develop their skills, but they also need to have a deeper understanding of the technology that advances their business. If they do not do this, they will not be able to make the most of the benefits of AI, and they may find themselves outdated.

At the social level, the next generation will need to be flexible and adapt to change. They must be willing to learn new skills to ensure they remain relevant and provide value as AI technology develops.

Establish transparency in all aspects of business: Transparency will be a key indicator of an organization's commitment and success in AI. Open communication about AI initiatives and their benefits can improve AI efficiency and morale and suppress fear among employees. Enterprise AI champions should also give priority to establishing transparency in their AI systems and processes. Artificial intelligence is complex and increasingly autonomous. Without visibility into AI, business leaders risk losing control of their business operations.

By ensuring transparency, business leaders can discover new opportunities and avoid potential risks before they cause serious problems or damage the company's customers, employees, or reputation.

Think beyond business process automation: Needless to say, organizations with well-defined AI strategies will have more successful AI plans. In the early stages of technology acceptance, it is natural to focus on automating existing business processes because it usually provides low-hanging fruit. However, automated substandard business processes may still be inefficient business processes, and AI just does it faster. In the spirit of ongoing digital transformation and innovation, AI initiatives should be viewed as opportunities to reinvent all aspects of the business.

Do not delay: Organizations across industries have realized the advantages of AI; those that deployed AI at an advanced level have significant benefits. Organizations that have not yet tried AI or planned their AI strategies will no doubt fall behind.

Significance of AI to business

According to Gartner, 30 percent of CIOs will include AI in their top five investment priorities, and 30 percent of new development projects will have AI components delivered by joint teams of data scientists and programmers. By 2025, that number will increase to more than 50 percent. Given the increasing priority, what should organizations and their shareholders expect from their CEOs in this world of AI?

Two concepts: preparedness and realization of value!

Center of an AI Strategy

When it is of AI implementation in the organization, the primary question is, who is at the center of AI strategy? While some might argue it's the CIO or Chief AI Officer (assuming there is one), COO, they can't be further away from the truth. None of the above. It is the CEO, who must be at the center of the AI strategy. Driving discussions on culture, strategies, shareholder and board approval, investments, talent, and more. If the CEO or business owner is pursuing AI as a strategic imperative, they are reducing the overall risks to the organization, according to Judson Althoff, EVP of Microsoft's Worldwide Commercial Business.

CEO's are at the heart of every business strategy. They must be there championing AI across the organization and ensuring employees' buy-in (which can be a challenging role while employees worry about the future of the jobs). CEOs need to align with IT teams to drive AI into both large and small projects. CEOs that acknowledge the potential of AI and

embrace it within their organizations are poised to succeed —
leapfrogging their competitors, transforming their industries.
In your organization, who truly owns the disruption plan if it
has one? Is it the CEO? How about the Chief Information
Officer? Or maybe the Chief Technology Officer? Ownership
can depend on the size or stage of the organization.

It all starts with business purpose and key performance
indicators (KPIs). Organizations and their leaders are
measured on performance against their alignment with
vision, mission, goals, strategies, and objectives. Before
considering the implications of artificial intelligence, the
CEOs must review financial, customer, employee,
community, and operational purposes over various
timeframes:

- Financial growth objectives for revenue, profitability,
  expense management and regulations. Customers at the
  center of each decision; without the customers and their
  identified needs, no business can succeed.
- Employee satisfaction indices, talent development,
  ethics. As CEO, you must be aware of and support the
  most innovative employees.
- Community-sustainability, charity, engagement —
  substantial words but are so crucial to your brand and
  the community you serve
- Operations – of its imperative that the operations teams'
  value cannot be overstated. Give them the right
  combination of leadership, technology, and process, and
  magic can happen.

Finding a CEO to lead an organization in the past was based
on skills and expertise in functions like leadership, finance,
operations, sales, and marketing. The CEOs of 2025 must be
able to guide their organization through the exponentially
rapid acceleration of AI and technological change to remain
competitive.

Expectations and Responsibilities of CIO

The CIOs are responsible for numerous strategies, including leading innovation, monitoring competition, and leading interactions with other functions. Their daily tasks include innovation labs, ecosystems, API intelligence/prediction, IoT, cloud, and open source strategy.

It is a responsibility of CIOs to remind CEOs and CFOs that digital disruption is a fast foe when it strikes and discusses the full list of ideas with them to see if different or more radical options could be tried. Top performers generate more digital revenue and create more digital processes. They should also:

- Be accountable for the maturity level of your digital positioning.
- Engage outside the IT department.
- Spend more time on executive leadership than IT delivery leadership.
- Anticipate the next wave of technology – they are present in the marketplace with technology leaders and understand how to leverage new tech.
- Prepare their organization for new tech technologies.

As you think about the roles that various C-suite players need to engage in for the AI strategy, consider these activities; Activities for the CEO like mergers, and acquisitions, legal action, funding sources, strategies like taking a private company, a spin-off, and replacing leaders; Activities for the CFOs and CHROs like pricing, hiring, firing, cannibalizing products, revenue recognition, investor relations, and outsourcing. Similarly, data analytics, media, communications, new targets, and awareness should be the responsibility of the chief marketing officer (CMOs). The sales leaders should be responsible for partnerships along with the sales channels. The product leaders in your organization should be made accountable for features, microservices, delivery, patents, and to some extent, even pricing. A Chief

---

Customer Officer in your organization should be focused on communications with customers, value, and advocacy for customers.

Facets of the AI Leader

AI leaders can foresee a more meaningful future, show organizational stakeholders what it can look like, and guide and enable their organizations to achieve the goal. In this way, they will instil sufficient progress and make society a "better" place to live – all of which are in line with fiduciary duties to organizations, stakeholders, and communities.

The future "cognitive company" will be completely different from what you know today. However, data is just a bunch of numbers, meaningless without context. Therefore, wise AI leaders should promote innovation, embrace collaboration between people and AI, and transform operations, markets, industries, and labor with new skills.

Artificial intelligence leaders will possess the following characteristics:

1. **Mobilizer:** Inspire people toward an envisioned future
2. **Social builder:** Insist on the interaction between people
3. **Humanist:** Value human creativity
4. **Mediator:** Unite humanity and AI in a joint mission
5. **Navigator:** Build a bridge in the AI ecosystem
6. **Explorer:** Use AI to enhance competitive advantage
7. **Sense maker:** Emphasize the clarity of AI design and process
8. **Architect:** Analysis, diagnose and, design
9. **Guardian:** Maintain the integrity of AI design and maintenance

---

Chapter 9

AI and Big Tech

****

"AI as being at the intersection of our ambitions. We want to democratize AI just like we brought information to your fingertips" – **Satya Nadella**

****

Large technology companies are leading in using artificial intelligence. Indeed, many smaller companies have only explored the use of AI in their businesses because they think they are losing ground to some of the other companies. Despite long-established anti-trust laws, large companies are becoming larger than ever before, dominating their industries in ways not seen since the 19th century. Indeed, these industry changes are happening so quickly that even the government has not been able to keep up, let alone small businesses that are looking to learn from big tech to stay competitive.

And still, that is exactly what these small businesses and their business leaders need to do: learn from big tech companies so they too can make the most out of AI. What is so brilliant about the behavior of big tech when it comes to AI is that they not only create programs that use artificial intelligence to market to their customers, but they have their own AI teams that use AI to analyze company data and make business decisions. Indeed, the ability of AI to make business decisions is regarded as one of the trends in AI that is most likely to shape business in the future.

The most obvious applications of AI in big tech companies may be the products of these companies' market that use artificial intelligence technology. Siri and Alexa are examples of artificial intelligence that millions if not billions of people use every day. Indeed, these products have exploded onto the market so quickly that many people have begun using them without knowledge of some of the concerns that their use entails.

Big tech companies have been able to use AI effectively, both in their businesses and in their products, because they have been at the forefront of AI research that has led to the development of new products. In truth, AI research is no longer sponsored primarily by governments, but by private industry, a picture of research that mainly has been in place for 30 years. Because these large companies are the sponsors of research in natural language processing (NLP) and artificial neural networks, they are usually the first to release products that make the most use of these technologies. In some cases, big tech companies acquire smaller companies that develop these technologies and incorporate them into their business.

Although big tech companies will always have an advantage when it comes to being financially positioned to sponsor AI research, it does not mean that smaller companies cannot make their way in the AI world. For example, a smaller company might have an exceptional, close-knit staff that is capable of developing a niche AI, which might be more difficult at a larger company that is being pulled in many different directions.

What this highlights here is the idea money represents only one part of the ability of businesses to engage in AI efforts. Perhaps the most crucial aspect of the AI effort is the brainpower. Large tech companies not only have the money to conduct AI research and invest in product development and marketing, but they are also able to attract teams of talented AI scientists and information scientists. These teams are essential to these companies to be able to develop AI and use it to best advantage in their business.

One of the lessons small businesses can learn from big companies is that employing talented AI teams can be their best competitive advantage against big companies. Large enterprises have machine learning teams that are involved in developing and using existing AI technology better. If a smaller company can attract such a team, then they can see the similar benefits that a larger company can. Smaller businesses can also be involved in creating products to market to customers, just as larger businesses can. Next, let's examine some of the ways larger companies use AI in their customer products.

Apple

Apple is one of the most innovative big tech companies today. Apple realized early on the way that mobile devices were converging with the Internet of Things (IoT), creating great potential for business. The Apple iPhone has been the most successful mobile phone ever, and its popularity has shown no signs of slowing. No doubt, the popularity of Apple has allowed the company to leverage some of its other products, a few of which use AI. Siri is perhaps the AI product that will be most familiar to people. Siri is a virtual assistant that serves as a component of iPhones, Apple Watches, iPads, and other Apple products. Siri uses natural language processing capabilities to understand language and completes tasks based on client requests. Siri truly represents the way that artificial intelligence software converges with IoT to create an AI world potentially. The fact that most devices nowadays have internet connectivity is what allows artificial intelligence to enter into the lives of modern-day people in ways that speculative fiction writers could never have imagined even 25 years ago.

Amazon

Amazon is, along with Google, Microsoft, and Facebook, one of the so-called Big Four technology companies. Amazon has revolutionized not only the way companies use AI, but also the way companies market products, and the way companies do business. In many ways, Amazon represents the business of the future. With its wide range of products available for purchase and its use of IoT to allow customers to purchase and receive products, Amazon represents a commercial enterprise that few businesses can realistically compete against.

However, Amazon gets a special mention here because of its Alexa product. Alexa has been used with other Amazon products, include Amazon Echo, and it can aid customers in a wide range of activities, including setting alarms, obtaining information, and playing music. Alexa represents what customers expect from commercially available AI products and the success that a business can achieve by understanding what customers want.

You know that customers want convenience. Living in an information age, AI can work together with IoT to provide men and women with information based solely on voice-based queries. Alexa has improved over time to take advantage of the AI technology to meet human needs (or rather, wants). Alexa has been integrated with a home automation system to allow users to control devices within their homes, including heating and cooling systems, alarms, and other devices. Smart homes represent another major trend in AI, and Alexa poises Amazon to be a part of this significant trend.

Microsoft

Microsoft is positioned to be a giant in artificial intelligence mainly because of the ubiquitous nature of its Windows operating system, and because of the massive amounts of data that it has access to. Microsoft is also the world's largest producer of software. Of all the companies mentioned on this list, Microsoft perhaps is the company that has been dealing with innovation and data management the longest. In addition, since Windows is an essential component of computers, Microsoft can be a player in AI that other companies perhaps cannot.

Microsoft uses AI in its business as a data management tool. It also markets AI to other large companies, like Carlsberg, the renowned beer manufacturer. Microsoft AI technology is being used by Carlsberg to "fingerprint" beer, which allows the company to develop new beer varieties and predict taste. This will enable Carlsberg to remain at the frontline of boutique brewing, allowing their business to stay competitive in an economic climate characterized by an increased number of players. Microsoft uses AI in ways that may only be known to them, making them still one of the most critical players in the data.

Google

Google is a big tech company that mainly came out of nowhere to dominate the internet. Google expanded from being a mere search engine to being arguably the world's most popular email provider and the most powerful (and popular) browser. This makes Google a rival of Microsoft, as Google now has access to user information that may exceed that of Microsoft. Again, data is vital as it not only allows companies to monitor their operations, but it provides training data for AI.

Google has many AI products that allow it to be a major player in artificial intelligence among big tech companies. It is at the forefront of natural language processing (NLP) capabilities of

AI. These language abilities of AI are used by Google Translate AI and by Google Home speakers, which function as a type of virtual assistant responding to commands. Google also has AI products that it develops and tailors to business clients. Like the other companies on this list, Google has machine learning teams that allow it to come up with new applications for AI. Again, Google can do this because it has access to so much data, not just useful information from searches and email, but data in the form of internet information pulled by its search engine.

Learning from AI usage at Big Tech

There is a lot of small businesses that can learn from big tech companies – most importantly, how they use AI. Companies like Facebook, General Electric, and Tesla are also at the forefront of AI, either because of one particular type of product that is trending in importance (like self-driving cars at Tesla), or because their access to data allows them to experiment with AI in novel ways.

That is precisely the takeaway about AI use at big tech companies. It is all about data. Companies like Microsoft and Google are so crucial in AI because data was not something peripheral to their business, but an essential component. These companies were in a position where they were unable to avoid data and its importance, recognizing early on how AI can be used to help them with data.

The key to small businesses learning from big companies is recognizing how they can better use their data. The days of ignoring data from company or equipment or customers are long in the past. Companies like Facebook and Apple do not ignore any of their data, and neither should you. Data provides insight to company leaders about changes they can incorporate to make their business better, whether those recommendations come from AI or analysts within the company.

The first step that many companies can take (if they want to be like the big tech companies) is to figure out how they can position their data so it can be accessed and used by AI. This may mean scanning documents and placing them on a cloud or investing in commercially available AI that is installed at your company and which can monitor various types of company data. Investing in AI as a small business is not as difficult as many business leaders think.

How AI Is Revolutionizing Industry

It can be said that artificial intelligence is one of the most changing factors in the industry today and may continue to do so in the future. Many think of AI in terms of the commercially available products that they use in their daily life. Siri and Alexa, in addition to smart home AI and other IoT devices that use AI, have become ubiquitous. But artificial intelligence is changing industry in ways that are invisible to many. These are things happening behind the scenes. Followings are few of the many Industries, where AI is changing rapidly: -

Banking

Artificial intelligence is redefining industries and changing the way businesses function. Every industry is assessing options and adopting ways to create value in the technology-driven world. The banking sector is witnessing ground-breaking changes— foremost being the rise in customer-centricity. To meet customer's expectations, banks have expanded their industry landscape to retail, IT, and telecom to enable services like mobile banking, e-banking, and real-time money transfers. These advancements have enabled customers to avail of most of the banking services at their fingertips anytime, anywhere.

Harnessing cognitive technology with artificial intelligence (AI) brings the advantage of digitization to banks and helps them meet the competition posed by FinTech players. About 32 percent of financial service providers are already using AI

---

technologies like Predictive Analytics, Voice Recognition, among others, according to joint research conducted by the National Business Research Institute, and Narrative Science.

Artificial intelligence is the future of banking as it brings the power of advanced data analytics to combat fraudulent transactions and improve compliance. AI algorithm accomplishes anti-money laundering activities in few seconds, which otherwise takes hours and days. AI also enables banks to manage huge volumes of data at record speed to derive valuable insights from it. Features such as AI bots, digital payment advisers, and biometric fraud detection mechanisms lead to a higher quality of services to a broader customer base. All this translates to increased revenue, reduced costs, and a boost in profits.

Agriculture

Agriculture is an industry that often falls under the radar in developed nations because it generally represents such a small percentage of GDP. Even in countries where agricultural products are major exports, agriculture is often not being perceived as being as significant as computer technology, aviation, heavy industry, or other industries that are more conspicuous. A few of the most challenging questions that farmers deal with are just how much they need to plant, how much they need to harvest as well as when they harvest. Agriculture is important, and AI has been changing this industry in dramatic ways. Agriculture is both a major industry and an economic foundation. AI in agriculture is helping farmers improve their efficiency and reduce hostile environmental impacts. The agriculture industry firmly and openly embraced AI into its practice to change the overall outcome.

Three keys ways in which AI is changing agriculture. It includes AI use in predictive analytics, crop and soil monitoring, and agricultural robots.

Agricultural Robots – Companies like Abundant Robotics, Agrobot, American Robotics, and many more are in developing and programming automated robots to handle basic agrarian tasks, such as harvesting crops in larger numbers and faster than manual labor.

Crop and Soil Monitoring – Companies like Arable, AgriData, and many more are using computer vision and deep learning algorithms to process data taken by drones and software-based technologies to monitor crop and soil health.

Predictive Analytics – Machine learning models are being developed to track and predict the various environmental impact on crop yields, such as weather changes.

Finally, AI can use drones and other agents (including computer programs) to monitor both crops and machinery in ways that would not have been possible before.

Healthcare Industry
Artificial intelligence makes lives easier for patients, doctors, and hospital administrators by performing tasks usually performed by humans, which requires less time and fraction of the cost. This is one of the fastest-growing industries in the world; the value of the artificial intelligence sector in 2014 was approximately USD 600 million and is expected to reach USD 150 billion by 2026. From finding new links between genetic codes or to driving artificial surgery-assisted robots, AI is reshaping and revitalizing modern healthcare through machines that predict, understand, learn, and act.

The most common aspect the health industry is using artificial intelligence for is recognizing types of cancer better than human doctors. The benefit of this is, of course, saving lives, but the truth of the matter is that artificial intelligence does not need to have you in the same room to make a diagnosis. Doctors insist they physically examine you, which means they often want you in the same space as themselves to give a

---

proper diagnosis. While AI is currently being used to improve the detection of malignant cancers, this technology is going to eventually come down the health industry ladder to the average individual. An individual simply needs to look into the mirror with their mouth open to see if there are white spots on the back of their throat to get an estimate of whether they have strep throat. Now, doctors often also insist on a saliva swab to ensure that the diagnosis is correct, but many diagnoses can be given in certain circumstances that only require a visual. For instance, a common cold is usually detected by looking at a patient and taking their vitals.

Here are a few ways; AI is saving lives:

Keeping well

One of the prime potential benefits of artificial intelligence is that it can help people stay healthy, so they don't need a doctor, or at least not so often. AI and the Internet of Medical Things (IoMT) in consumer health applications are already helping people. Technology applications and apps, e.g., fit bit, encourage individuals to adopt healthier behaviors, and help them actively manage healthy lifestyles. They enable consumers to control health and well-being.

Early Detection

Artificial intelligence has been used to detect early diseases more accurately, such as cancer. According to the American Cancer Society, a large number of mammograms can produce erroneous results, resulting in 50 percent healthy women detected falsely to have cancer. Using AI can increase the speed of examination and translation of mammograms by 30 times, with an accuracy rate of 99percent, thereby reducing unnecessary biopsies.

Consumer wearables and other medical devices combined with AI are also being used to monitor early heart disease, allowing doctors and other caregivers to better monitor and detect early and treatable life-threatening events.

Diagnosis

IBM's Watson for Health is helping healthcare organizations apply cognitive technology to unlock vast amounts of health data and power diagnosis. Watson can review and store medical information of every medical journal around the world, symptoms, and case studies of treatment and respond faster than anyone. Google's DeepMind Health is working with clinicians, researchers, and patients to solve real-world healthcare issues. This technology combines machine learning and system neuroscience and builds powerful general-purpose learning algorithms into neural networks that mimic the human brain.

Treatment

In addition to scanning health records to help providers identify patients with chronic diseases that may be at risk of adverse episodes, AI can also help clinicians adopt a more comprehensive disease management approach, better coordinate care plans, and help patients to better manage and comply with their long-term medical treatment plan.

Robots have been used in medicine for more than three decades. They range from simple laboratory robots to highly sophisticated surgical robots, which can either help human surgeons or perform operations on their own. In addition to surgery, they are also used for repetitive tasks in hospitals and laboratories, rehabilitation, physical therapy, and support for chronically ill patients.

AI in Education

Artificial intelligence in education is not just science fiction. A study found that 34 hours of language education on Duolingo's app is equivalent to the entire university semester. American Education Industry Report says artificial intelligence in American education is expected to grow by 47.5 percent from 2017 to 2021.

Artificial intelligence systems are being used to tailor and personalize learning for each student. Through ultra-personalized functions are based on machine learning, AI systems are used to develop customized learning materials for students, based on their abilities, preferred learning modes and experiences. It is estimated that by 2024, more than 47 percent of learning management tools will be enabled by AI functions. Educators will no longer need teachers to create a single course for all students but will provide enhanced intellectual help to use the same core courses to provide various materials to meet the specific needs of each student.

AI is changing education in many ways, including distance learning, chatbots, school recruitment, and outreach, classroom or dorm room learning, administrative tasks, feedbacks for both educators and students, tutoring students, grading, tailoring of educational software to student needs.

The truth is because artificial intelligence can use whatever data you give it, the possibilities of AI in education are almost endless. For example, AI programs may be able to review student data and make recommendations on areas in which students need improvement based on a more nuanced understanding of the data than the teachers have. AI can even recommend changes in instruction based on student's performance in certain areas. E-learning is getting popular during Covid-19, wherein distance education is being implemented to maintain social distance. Students can learn and practice speech or presentation through virtual reality

---

software to feel like attending an actual class. Educators are using the smartboard to teach and interact online and class students at the same time. Also, students and educators can use AI-powered online assessments to evaluate the understanding of students.

Media and Entertainment

The media and entertainment industry are at the crossover of rapid transformation, focusing on digital media. Artificial intelligence is increasingly becoming an engine that can drive more vibrant and more realistic experiences in media and entertainment, from video games to movies and more.

Machine learning and experimental APIs have found a place in the media and entertainment industry. As with other areas of business, a significant area for entertainment to make use of AI is in predictive analytics.

Predictive analytics in the context of entertainment can mean many things, but this would include predicting consumer behavior to suggest certain types of products, like films, digital programming, games, sports, or TV shows. AI can also be used to market products directly to customers using the web or app-based utilities. AI of this type tracks user data to make tailored recommendations.

AI can also be involved in preparing products for release using deep learning. For example, AI can be included in video editing, syncing audio, and video, and in image analysis for entertainment purposes. As you have seen, machine learning can play a dominant role in language processing and translation, and this can be very relevant in the entertainment industry.

Transportation

AI is revolutionizing the transportation industry in the most significant way with the invention of the self-driving car. Although self-driving automobiles have been in development

---

since the 1970s, it has only been recently that advancements in image analysis, machine learning, and semantic segmentation have allowed self-driving to be a safe endeavor that human beings can expect to see in the near future. Indeed, navigation systems powered by AI are already in place both in automobiles and in aviation. The tasks that AI has in self-driving involves deep learning. AI in self-driving cars needs to be engaged in multiple complex algorithms at the same time, including recognizing signs in the environment, identifying markers on the road, awareness of other vehicles and pedestrians, using location and weather data to guide actions, responding to input from a human driver, and physically moving the automobile. The fact that self-driving cars are being developed by companies like Tesla and others can represent one of the great achievements of modern-day machine learning. The use of AI in transportation demonstrates why the market has surged and why companies should adopt the technology.

Self-driving vehicles
One of the most breakthrough applications of artificial intelligence is self-driving cars. The concept of self-driving cars, once a science fiction fantasy, has now become a reality.

Automatic taxis in Tokyo have already opened. However, for safety reasons, so far, the driver sits in the car to control the taxi in emergency situations. The manufacturers of such automated taxis believe the technology will reduce the cost of taxi services, which will help increase public transportation in remote areas.

Similarly, American Logistics has begun to use self-driving trucks. According to McKinsey's report, 65 percent of the world's cargo is transported by truck. With the advent of self-driving trucks, maintenance and management costs will be reduced by 45 percent.

At present, most companies are still running their pilot projects to make driverless cars flawless and safe for passengers. With the development of technology, self-driving cars will gain the trust of the public and become the mainstream in the consumer field.

Traffic management

One of the most significant traffic problems people face every day is traffic jams. AI can also solve this problem. Sensors and cameras implanted all over on the road can collect the large voluminous amount of traffic information. Then these send data to the cloud, where the big data analysis and AI-based systems analyze and reveal the traffic patterns. Valuable insights, such as traffic forecasts, can be collected from data processing. Commuters can get essential details, such as traffic forecasts, accidents, or road jams. Besides, people can be notified of the shortest route to their destination to help them travel without traffic hassles. In this way, AI can not only reduce unnecessary traffic but also improve road safety and reduce waiting time.

Delay predictions

Today, another serious problem faced by air transport is flight delays. According to a study by researchers at the University of California, Berkeley, the loss due to flight delays is estimated to be USD 39 billion in the United States. In addition to economic losses, flight delays also hurt passengers' flight experience. Negative experiences during the flight may destroy the value of the transportation company, leading to an increase in customer churn. To overcome these problems, artificial intelligence is here to help the air transport industry.

Using data lake technology and computer vision, the industry can provide passengers with superior service, thereby reducing passengers' waiting time and improving their travel experience. Anything from bad weather to technical failure may cause flight delays, so it is essential to update flight information to passengers in advance to eliminate unnecessary waiting time. With the help of a computer vision system, the aircraft can be continuously monitored to reduce inadvertent downtime.

In addition, artificial intelligence and machine learning components will process real-time aircraft data, historical records, and weather information. On-the-spot calculations will reveal hidden patterns, which can help the air transport industry gather useful insights into other possibilities that may cause flight delays and cancellations. This data can be forwarded to commuters, which can help them plan their schedule accordingly.

Drone taxis

Drone taxi is one of the most exciting and innovative AI applications in transportation. Pilotless helicopters present a unique solution that can solve carbon emissions, eliminate traffic congestion, and reduce the need for expensive infrastructure. Besides, drone taxis will help people reach their destinations faster, thereby minimizing travel time.

The ever-increasing population puts enormous pressure on city planners, requiring them to ensure wise urban planning and building infrastructure without conceding on declining resources. Drone taxis can indeed be a real way to solve all the problems these city planners are trying to solve. A demonstration of a self-driving aircraft recently demonstrated intelligent smart air mobility in China flying 17 passengers for the first time, which is a good indication of similar future applications.

AI Platforms to Build Modern Application

Amazon AI Services

As Amazon is rapidly putting companies out of business, so is AWS, which is so dominant as a platform that there's almost nothing else that comes to mind. The same is true of Amazon AI services, which are full of benefits. AWS has some exciting services like: -

https://aws.amazon.com/machine-learning/ai-services/

Amazon Comprehend: Amazon Comprehend is a natural language processing (NLP) service that uses machine learning to find insights and relationships in a text. This can help you understand a lot of text (unstructured data). One use case is to mine existing customer support chat records and find satisfaction over a period, mainly focused on customers and the most frequently used keywords.

Amazon Forecast: Today, companies use everything from simple spreadsheets to complex financial planning software to try to accurately predict future business outcomes, like product requirements, resource requirements, or financial performance. These tools build forecasts by looking at historical data series (called time series data). Amazon

---

Forecast is a fully managed service that uses machine learning to provide highly accurate forecasts.

Amazon Lex: Amazon Lex is a service for building conversational interfaces into any application using voice and text. It provides advanced deep learning capabilities, including automatic speech recognition (ASR) and natural language understanding (NLU), for converting speech to text to recognize the intent of the text, enabling developers to build a highly engaging user experience with realistic conversational interactions. With Amazon Lex, developers can now use the same deep learning technology like Amazon Alexa, allowing them to build sophisticated natural language conversation robots quickly and easily ("chat robots").

Amazon Personalize: Based on more than 20 years of recommendation experience, Amazon Personalize enables you to increase customer engagement by providing personalized product and content recommendations and targeted marketing promotions. Through machine learning, Amazon Personalize creates higher quality recommendations for your websites and applications.

Google AI Services

Like Amazon's service, Google also has a cloud service around artificial intelligence. The following is a screenshot of the content of interest to developers:

AI and Machine Learning

AI Building Blocks

AI building blocks
Easily infuse AI into applications with custom or pre-trained models.

AutiML
Cusom machine learning model training and development.

Vision AI
Cusom and pre-trained models to detect emotion, text, more.

Video AI
Video classification and recognition using machine learning.

Cloud Natural Language
Sentiment analysis and classification of unstructured text.

Cloud Translation
Language detection, translation, and glossary support.

Media Translation (beta)
Add dynamic audio translation directly to your content and applications.

Text-to-Speech
Speech synthesis in 180+ voices and 30+ languages.

Speech-to-Text
Speech recognition and transcription supporting 120 languages.

Dialogflow
Conversation applications and systems development suite.

AutoML Tables (beta)
Service for training ML models with structured data.

Cloud Inference API (alpha)
Quickly run large-scale correlations over typed time-seriec datasets.

Recommendations AI (beta)
Deliver highly personalized product recommendations at scale.

https://cloud.google.com/products

You can use Google's AI service in two ways. The first method is to use the model that Google has trained and then apply it to your product. The second method is the so-called AutoML service, which can automate multiple intermediate stages of machine learning, thereby helping full-stack developers with less ML expertise to build and train models quickly.

H2O

H2O is an open-source platform for machine learning, used by big names in the Fortune 500. The foremost idea is to make cutting-edge AI research reach the public, rather than leaving it in the hands of rich companies. The H2O platform provides a variety of products, such as:

• **H2O:** A primary platform for exploring and using machine learning.

• **Sparkling Water:** Formally integrated with Apache Spark for large data sets.

• **H2O4GPU:** GPU accelerated version of the H2O platformH2O also tailors' solutions for companies, including:

Driverless AI: No, driverless AI has nothing to do with self-driving cars. It comes more from Google's AutoML product line - most AI/ML stages are automated, making tools for development easier and faster.

Paid support: As an enterprise, you can't wait to ask GitHub questions and hope to get answers soon. If time is money, H2O will provide paid support and consulting for large companies.

IBM Watson

Thanks to Watson, IBM is one of the best AI engines. It uses modern innovative technology in machine learning, which can make the model learn more information with fewer data. Developers can choose to build new models from scratch, or they can use Watson APIs and pre-trained solutions to support existing applications. IBM Watson is different because it can learn from small data sets. IBM believes that what makes the difference is the quality of the data, not the quantity.

IBM Watson includes multiple enterprise-level AI services, applications, and tools. These tools include Watson's Assistant like Watson Studio, AI OpenScale, Watson Discovery, natural language understanding, news discovery, knowledge Studio, language translator, natural language classifier, personality insight, tone analyzer, visual recognition, and speech to text.

Also, Watson allows companies to integrate their services into Salesforce and Box. Salesforce integration can help companies provide AI-based solutions and make quick and informed decisions across services and sales. The Box integration aims to automate the structure of content, unleash hidden value, and automate workflow in the cloud.

Chapter 10

The Future of AI

****

"By 2025, an estimated 95% of customer interactions will be supported by AI technology."

-FORBES

****

The final goal of artificial intelligence (AI)—that a machine can have a type of *general* intelligence (or strong AI) like a human's—is one of the most ambitious ever proposed by science. You are inching towards *general* intelligence (or strong AI), and it is expected that by 2050, you will have *general* intelligence (or strong AI) in place.

Remember those Hollywood science fiction movies that you watched during childhood. These may not be 'fiction' for long. Artificial intelligence is the future, and as crazy as it may sound, the future could no longer be in your hands, and it might be in your machine's hands. Your brains are focused on developing AI, which is taking over faster than you can imagine.

Sundar Pichai, the CEO of Google, once said, *"everything in Google is going to be AI centered, which could mean that AI will create numerous job opportunities that will require creativity, critical thinking skills, and much more."*

You use gadgets that are intelligent and make your everyday tasks easy. For example, Alexa can remind you about your daily appointments, keep a check on your grocery list, play your favorite music when you need, read the news, and even play some brain games! It is like a human companion; however, it is not human but has human-like capabilities. There are restaurants where robots serve food for humans.

A trillion dollars is a massive sum of money. By 2022, the Internet of Things (IoT) is expected to achieve that level of savings for industry and individuals alike through transparent and immersive experiences, according to Gartner.

So, what does the present have in store for AI? Well, you start with the "year of the voice." People are increasingly turning from texting to talking. With the advent of hyper accuracy in voice recognition (think back a decade when your voice recognition software was less than 50 percent accurate), voice input systems are now viable. Alexa from Amazon has become prolific in advertisements and television shows where it's featured interacting with homeowners. Alexa is expanding "her" service offering beyond dimming the lights, playing music and offering restaurant recommendations.

Organizations like Adobe and Salesforce are branching into omnichannel capabilities with voice moving to the forefront. Customer service contact centers are leveraging greater, deeper upfront interactions with more human-like responses, incorporating emotional understanding such as customer frustration. Most of the big companies have started virtual assistants with the help of AI. Once vented to the assistant for the specific question, it will move you to a human agent—a great combination of automation and human interaction.

Organizations have already started using voice and speech recognition technologies to frustrate a fraudster. Bank and telephone companies are leveraging this biometric technology. Using only a small sample of words of speech, voice biometrics can identify you, including whether the speech is live or not, so fraudsters cannot leverage recordings in the case of a breach. HSBC became the first bank to practice voice recognition in products released to customers. As per the bank, mobile banking customers no longer need to remember passwords and other data to access their accounts. The uniqueness of your voice now serves to introduce you to your banker as the "Real You" as the world continues to experience record levels of hacking, your real-time voice maybe your best safety measures.

Brands like Best Buy and Walmart entered into relationships with Google Home and Amazon Alexa to increase the adoption of voice-based software solutions and services. Successful marketers are thinking like those in customer care in dealing with a variety of customers as the point of contact professionals. Once organizations gain customers' trust, they can begin achieving cost-efficient voice solutions. People have started using Google assistant extensively for google search, news, setting up an alarm, sending a text, setting up reminders, etc. through voice.

Elon Musk's Predictions
Elon Musk, the co-founder of OpenAI and the CEO of SpaceX and Tesla, made a series of predictions regarding the future. His predictions ranged from the eventuality of pervasive electric and autonomous vehicles to tunnel transportation to Mars landings. Tesla production and delivery are ramping up, SpaceX launches are commonplace, and Hyperloop competitions for tunneling have abounded. Its clear Musk has a wildly substantial impact on the world, and his predictions suggest a future of more of the same.

Cars becoming "all-electric" in 2019 doesn't seem so far-fetched, but aircraft and ships as well? Musk thinks so, "with

---

the ironic exception of rockets." Getting back to cars, he says half of all cars will be electric by 2027.

Picture yourself in 2028. If you're still driving around in your fossil-fuel engined Mustang GT, will people look at you as if you're riding a horse? Musk thinks so. Maybe you're too sentimental to give up that "horse."

Elon Musk has a very robust viewpoint about AI taking jobs, and he agrees with those who say it will make humans jobless. The billionaire entrepreneur said at NGA:

"Of course, there will be work interruptions. Because what is going to happen is robots will be able to do everything better than us. ... I mean all of us."

How about that vacation to Mars? You'll have to wait until at least 2025 when the first human travelers are predicted to travel to, and land on Mars, according to Musk speaking at the International Astronautical Congress. If you'd like to live in Montreal but work in Toronto, Canada, it takes about 5 hours to do the "commute." It can take over an hour just to get to Toronto from a suburb of the same city. Yet with a Hyperloop tunnel, that time frame could be 25 minutes from Montreal. Not bad. Getting out of bed in your Montreal home at seven and having your morning coffee at your desk in Toronto before 8 o'clock. With a network of tunnels, North America could be your playground if you use Hyperloop to get to and from work.

Sounds generally positive, does it not? Well, "not" would be the correct answer. Artificial intelligence is more dangerous than nuclear weapons, if not regulated, will end human lives. At the National Governors Association held in July 2017, Musk expressed his fears of AI by saying:

"I have access to the most cutting-edge AI, and I think people should be concerned about it. Artificial intelligence is the major risk for the survival of human civilization, but it is not

the case with traffic accidents, aircraft crashes, drug problems, or bad food-of course. They are harmful to a set of people in society."

Ultramodern Romance

Imagine you are a woman or a man seeking romance in this new world. You say "date," and your soul band shines. The personal AI assistant embedded in the band starts working. The night before, your compassionate AI searched the cloud for three possible dates. Now, your Soul band will project a high-definition hologram for each of them. If it recommends No. 3, a poetry-loving master plumber with a smoky look and you say "yes," the AI will open the door to greet the incarnation of men or women to determine the time of your actual meeting. Perhaps your AI will also mention which flower you like for future reference.

After years of experience, you may find that your AI is better than you at choosing your partner. It may predict that if you divorce your husband, you will be happier, and it may turn out to be true. Once you decide to leave him or her, your AI will negotiate with the soon-to-be ex-husband, write a divorce agreement, and then "tour" a dozen apartments in the cloud to finds the right apartment for you.

Your AI can help you in all aspects of your life. It will remember every conversation you ever had, every invention sketch you made on a napkin, and every business meeting you ever attended. It will also be familiar with the inventions of millions of others-scanning patent applications over hundreds of years-and reading all commercial books written since the Franklin era. When you bring up a new idea for your business, your AI will immediately cross-reference it with the concept introduced at a meeting in Singapore or Dubai a few minutes ago. It's like having a team of geniuses- Einstein for physics, Steve Jobs for business—anytime, anywhere.

AI will remember your favorite author and mention her surname "Austen," which will connect you with the Chinese service, which spent hours reading everything written by Jane Austen. It can imitate her style well to produce new novels that are not different from the old ones.

Live Long and Prosper

Imagine your multiple lives: when you were 25, you were a climber; when you were 55, you were a judo athlete; when you were 95, you were a storyteller; at 155, you were a poet. Extending human life is one of the dreams of the post-curious world. AI will do their best to keep you healthy. Sensors at home will continuously test your breathing to find early signs of cancer, and nanorobots will swim in your blood, consuming the plaque in your brain and dissolving blood clots to prevent strokes or heart attacks.

Your soul band, which helps you to find your lover, will serve as a medical assistant taking 24/7 calls. It will monitor your immune response, proteins, and metabolites, and have a long-term understanding of your health so doctors can accurately understand the condition of the body.

When you are sick, your doctor will accept your symptoms and match them to millions of cases over hundreds of years.

By 2065, artificial intelligence will completely change our genome. Scientists will be able to edit human DNA in a way the editor corrects a bad manuscript, cut off the inferior part, and replace it with a healthy and beneficial gene. Only a super-intelligent system would map out surprisingly complex gene mutation interactions, thus generating genius pianists or star second basemen.

Humans will look back at the beginning of the 21st century, the way people look back at the 18th century: the period of disease and disaster, children and loved ones shrouded in disease. By 2065, humans will be on the verge of getting rid of the biology that created them.

Big Brother

Imagine that by 2065, artificial intelligence will help the nation-state to function. Countries that have adopted AI to assist governments are thriving. Nigeria and Malaysia will have accredited institutions to vote on behalf of their owners, and corruption and mismanagement will disappear. In just a few years, citizens will grow into trusting and accrediting institutions, which can advise leaders with the best economic development path and defend them with suggestions on the number of soldiers. The treaty will be negotiated by AI trained on diplomatic data sets.

In Lagos, "civil rights" drones will fly over police pods rushing to the crime scene-one AI will monitor the other AI to protect humans. All police stations in Lagos or Kuala Lumpur will have their own polygraph AI, which will be reliable, making crooked police a thing of the past. Hovering over the Kuala Lumpur bridge will be a "psychological drone" monitoring the suicide jumper. Super intelligent machines will not evolve into the terrible Skynet of the Terminator movie, but will be friendly and curious to us; however, imagine you are a citizen of an authoritarian country like North Korea – you will be deep in the dark side of AI. Political prison camps will be a thing of the past. Physical confinement won't be the focus. The police will already know your criminal record, your DNA composition, and your sexual orientation. Surveillance drones will track your every move. Your Soul band will record every conversation you have and your biometric response to anti-government advertising, and it will flash on the video screen at unexpected moments.

The right to privacy will disappear around 2060. Won't be able to tell right from wrong. When the government has AI, it can invade every part of your survival. The call you receive may be about the weather that your aunt Jackie made to chat, or the state robot wanting to know your true thoughts about the great leader.

5G

Imagine connectivity speeds of 100 times faster than the widely available 4G standard today. Download times reduced substantially, and full movies download in seconds and incredible responsiveness for your applications. Telecom companies are in a race to become your 5G provider, billions in 5G infrastructure spending are happening right now to offer subscribers lightning-fast connectivity

So what is 5G? It is the 5th generation of mobile networks, a massive change from 4G LTE as measured by latency (the time is taken for devices to respond to each other over the wireless network). 3G network's typical response time was 100 milliseconds, 4G is approximately 30 milliseconds, and 5G is predicted to be as low as one millisecond.

For AI-powered offerings augmented with 5G, think autonomous vehicles and the ability to increase the connection speed of data flowing between the vehicle and data sources. This will be more necessary in areas where more reliable coverage is needed, including machine downtime and IoT sensors. AI and 5G are a marriage made in heaven. Smart city technologies will depend upon the combination of Al and 5G speed.

Quantum Computers

Today's fastest supercomputer (while writing this book) is called Summit and is housed at Oak Ridge National Lab in Tennessee. Summit is currently being used to run deep learning algorithms at a billion operations per second speed to address one of the primary challenges of our time, climate change.

Quantum computing operates or is expected to operate with all levels of artificial intelligence: narrow general, super-intelligence, or compassionate artificial superintelligence. Yet quantum computing is quite fragile and sensitive to

---

environmental noise outside the device, like temperature (-460 degrees Fahrenheit). It requires highly specialized techniques to preserve the quantum state. It's unlikely the majority of organizations would ever have a quantum computer, and preferably the environment would be more like a cloud system with clients buying access. Companies like Intel, IBM, Microsoft, and Google are pursuing Quantum computing operations with 5 to 50 qubits capabilities (as measured by units called qubits).

You may have heard or read about quantum computers and their potential to support the processing needs of machine learning, neural networks, and algorithms. Artificial intelligence, as it approaches General AI (higher level super-intelligent systems), requires many things, including vast amounts of processing power. Yet we are still years away from a full-fledged true quantum computer.

The 5G and quantum-powered future, though, is coming

Indeed, artificial intelligence has always been one of the most astounding technological innovations of mankind. However, although you have seen every amazing invention so far, it should be noted that you just scratched the surface of AI, and there are still many things to be explored. The AI applications mentioned in the book demonstrate the possibilities and opportunities that the technology can provide. Imagine just how amazing and exciting the future driven by artificial intelligence will be!

Finally, either embrace artificial intelligence or get eliminated by it.

_____

May I Ask You A Small Favor?

At the outset, I sincerely thank you for taking the time to read this book. You could have chosen any other book, but you took mine, and I appreciate your gesture. I hope it was an enjoyable learning experience and may be helpful in understanding artificial intelligence and its applications.

If anything in this book resonated with you, **I'd love it if you would leave a review on Amazon**. Reviews may not matter to big-name authors, but they're a tremendous help for new authors like me.

Feel free to get in touch with me at toajitjha@gmail.com if you have any specific queries on anything related to this book or in general. I love to read emails from my readers.

References

https://computer.howstuffworks.com/boolean.htm
https://animalventures.com/blog/what-is-machine-learning-a-beginners-guide/
http://www.iamwire.com/2017/07/algorithms-machine-learning-engineers/155436
https://techiethoughtss.wordpress.com/2020/01/06/machine-learning-introduction/
https://xccelerate.co/blog/machine-learning-types-examples/
https://www.oreilly.com/library/view/principles-of-data/9781785887918/ch10s04.html
https://www.datasciencecentral.com/profiles/blogs/top-9-machine-learning-applications-in-real-world
https://news.sap.com/2016/01/hr-runs-simple-with-innovations-in-travel-and-expense-management/
https://racksimply.com/examples-of-artificial-intelligence-today/
https://roboticsbiz.com/top-16-real-life-examples-and-use-of-machine-learning/
https://medium.com/app-affairs/9-applications-of-machine-learning-from-day-to-day-life-112a47a429d0
https://insights.daffodilsw.com/blog/9-machine-learning-examples-from-day-to-day-life
https://www.office.xerox.com/latest/855BR-01.PDF
https://chromium.googlesource.com/external/github.com/tensorflow/tensorflow/+/r0.7/tensorflow/g3doc/resources/dims_types.md
https://en.wikipedia.org/wiki/PyTorch
https://www.advancedsciencenews.com/artificial-astronomers/
https://centramic.com/artificial-intelligence-applications/
Tripathy, Mayank, and Deepak Shrivastava. "Designing and Implementation of an Efficient Fingerprint Recognition System Using Minutia F......"
International Journal of Science, Engineering , Indian Association .., June 2015, p
http://cs229.stanford.edu/proj2017/final-reports/5244211.pdf
https://blog.usejournal.com/a-quick-introduction-to-k-nearest-neighbors-algorithm-62214cea29c7
https://journalofbigdata.springeropen.com/articles/10.1186/s40537-019-0219-y
http://www.global-engage.com/life-science/deep-learning-in-digital-pathology/
https://dev.to/victoromondi1997/artificial-intelligence-vs-data-science-vs-machine-learning-3636
https://journals.aom.org/doi/10.5465/AME.1998.254975
https://blog.usejournal.com/a-quick-introduction-to-k-nearest-neighbors-algorithm-62214cea29c7
https://builtin.com/data-science/unsupervised-learning-python
https://blogs.oracle.com/datascience/introduction-to-k-means-clustering
https://www.guru99.com/deep-learning-tutorial.html
https://docs.aws.amazon.com/sagemaker/latest/dg/reinforcement-learning.html
https://becominghuman.ai/10-powerful-examples-of-ai-applications-553f7f062d9f
https://centramic.com/artificial-intelligence-applications/
https://dev.to/victoromondi1997/artificial-intelligence-vs-data-science-vs-machine-learning-3636

https://www.javatpoint.com/pytorch-prediction-and-linear-class
Halverson, Grace. "Benefits of AI and Machine Learning for Cloud Security." IT Pro ,
Dennis Publishing Ltd., Jan. 2019, p. n/a.
https://journals.aom.org/doi/10.5465/AME.1998.254975
https://www.vphrase.com/blog/applications-of-ai-in-the-media-entertainment-
industry/
https://elearningindustry.com/ai-is-changing-the-education-industry-5-ways
https://www.lexalytics.com/lexablog/ai-in-education-present-future-ethics
https://centramic.com/artificial-intelligence-applications/
http://oneindiaonepeople.com/has-india-woken-up-to-artifical-intelligence/
https://elitedatascience.com/machine-learning-algorithms
https://www.guru99.com/supervised-machine-learning.html
https://medium.com/machine-learning-bites/machine-learning-supervised-
lear.......https://www.educba.com/svm-algorithm/
http://cs229.stanford.edu/proj2017/final-reports/5244211.pdf
Tripathy, Mayank, and Deepak Shrivastava. "Designing and Implementation of an
Efficient Fingerprint Recognition System Using Minutia Feature and KNN
Classifier." International Journal of Science, Evol. 5, no. 6, ..., June 2015, p. 166.
https://journalofbigdata.springeropen.com/articles/10.1186/s40537-019-0219-y
https://towardsdatascience.com/understanding-adaboost-2f94f22d5bfe
https://www.youtube.com/playlist?list=PLPXKwZqdJ5n1q2B1sb1CoH4pdY4rgIh3
https://www.aithority.com/news/top-10-countries-and-cities-by-number-of-cctv-
cameras/
https://www.dataversity.net/data-surveillance-monitoring-spying-personal-
privacy-data-gathering-world/
https://www.edureka.co/blog/cognitive-ai/
https://www.esri.com/en-us/arcgis/products/spatial-analytics-data-
science/capabilities/spatial-analysis
https://www.clarabridge.com/customer-experience-dictionary/text-analytics
https://www.capterra.com/text-mining-software/
https://www.simplilearn.com/introduction-to-tensorflow-tutorial
https://www.infoworld.com/article/3278008/what-is-tensorflow-the-machine-
learning-library-explained.html
https://www.infoworld.com/article/3278008/what-is-tensorflow-the-machine-
learning-library-explained.html
https://www.inetservices.com/blog/what-is-tensorflow-the-machine-learning-
library-explained/
https://pypi.org/project/Keras/
https://en.wikipedia.org/wiki/Keras
https://blog.adafruit.com/2020/05/01/installing-pytorch-on-a-raspberry-pi-3b-
piday-raspberrypu-python-raspberry_pi/
https://docs.rstudio.com/resources/tensorflow/
https://stackshare.io/stackups/cuda-vs-pytorch
https://www.researchoptimus.com/article/what-is-time-series-analysis.php
https://masomomsingi.com/cifa-financial-mathematics-revision-kit-for-kasneb-
exams/
https://masomomsingi.com/cifa-financial-mathematics-revision-kit-for-kasneb-
exams/
https://www.researchoptimus.com/article/what-is-time-series-analysis.php

---

https://www.researchoptimus.com/article/what-is-time-series-analysis.php
https://www.guru99.com/nlp-tutorial.html
https://www.tutorialspoint.com/artificial_intelligence_with_python/artificial_inte
lligence_with_python_natural_language_processing.htm
https://searchbusinessanalytics.techtarget.com/definition/natural-language-
processing-NLP
https://data-flair.training/blogs/ai-natural-language-processing/
https://www.guru99.com/nlp-tutorial.html
https://towardsdatascience.com/your-guide-to-natural-language-processing-nlp-
48ea2511f6e1
https://opendatascience.com/an-introduction-to-natural-language-processing-nlp/
https://www.learningspiral.ai/computer-vision.php
https://medium.com/vsinghbisen/what-is-computer-vision-in-machine-learning-
and-ai-how-it-works-b8bc70aef3c7
https://www.skyfilabs.com/blog/how-to-develop-a-computer-vision-project
https://algorithmia.com/blog/introduction-to-computer-vision
https://www.researchoptimus.com/article/what-is-time-series-analysis.php
https://medium.com/machine-learning-bites/machine-learning-supervised-
learning-algorithms-summary-76adc41b8ecc
https://www.houseofbots.com/news-detail/4006-1-strengths-and-weaknesses-of-
modern-machine-learning-algorithms,-everyone-should-know
http://uc-r.github.io/gbm_regression
https://medium.com/@aravanshad/gradient-boosting-versus-random-forest-
cfa3fa8f0d80
https://opendatascience.com/an-introduction-to-natural-language-processing-nlp/
https://www.ibaroody.com/manufacturing-factories-machines-learning-software-
sales-training/
https://www.capterra.com/p/151928/Text-Analyzer/alternatives/
https://www.researchoptimus.com/article/what-is-time-series-analysis.php
https://www.researchoptimus.com/article/what-is-time-series-analysis.php
https://www.dremio.com/tutorials/multi-source-time-series-data-prediction-with-
python-dremio/
https://news.developer.nvidia.com/nature-supercharge-your-research-with-a-gpu/
https://stackshare.io/stackups/scikit-learn-vs-scipy
https://www.findbestopensource.com/product/kristofferc-tensors-jl
https://github.com/rstudio/tensorflowsemantastic.com:8087.
http://semantastic.com:8087/wiki/Notes/PythonToolSets?format=txt
https://github.com/reddyprasade/Learn_Pytorch
https://haosdent.gitbooks.io/tensorflowdocument/content/resources/dims_types.
html
https://artificial-intelligence.financesonline.com/
https://news.developer.nvidia.com/nature-supercharge-your-research-with-a-gpu/
https://www.analyticsvidhya.com/blog/2015/11/quick-introduction-boosting-
algorithms-machine-learning/
https://www.educba.com/adaboost-algorithm/
https://blog.ephorie.de/understanding-adaboost-or-how-to-turn-weakness-into-
strength
https://ponisha.ir/project/92586/%D8%AA%D8%B1%D8%AC%D9%85%D9%8

https://www.accenture.com/in-en/insights/artificial-intelligence...
https://www.accenture.com/in-en/insight-artificial-intelligence-future-growth]
https://softwarecontractsolutions.com/the-true-costs-and-roi-of-implementing-ai-in-the-enterprise/
https://emeritus.kellogg.northwestern.edu/artificial-intelligence/index.php
Blog. https://blog.vsoftconsulting.com/blog/page/18
[https://www.accenture.com/in-en/insights/artificial-intelligence/ai-governance-support-innovation
https://searchenterpriseai.techtarget.com/definition/AI-governance]
https://www.sas.com/en_us/insights/articles/big-data/5-machine-learning-mistakes.html
https://www.houseofbots.com/news-detail/3887-1-what-mistakes-usually-done-by-organizations-while-deploying-machine-learning
Polyzois, Dimos, et al. "Poor Indoor Air Quality, Mold Exposure....., Mar. 2016, p. 20.
https://www.accenture.com/in-en/services/ai-artificial-intelligence-index
https://cloudblogs.microsoft.com/industry-blog/en-gb/technetuk/2020/01/23/an-intro-to-ai-and-the-ai-builder/
https://tallyfy.com/adkar-model/
https://www.accenture.com/us-en/insights/artificial-intelligence/artificial-intelligence-explained-executives
https://www.fzi.de/en/news/news/detail-en/artikel/kuenstliche-intelligenz-bestimmt-die-lebens-und-arbeitswelt-von-morgen/
https://www.clickz.com/how-to-yield-higher-marketing-roi-coupling-smart-systems-with-smart-b2b-social-media-strategies/27822/
https://economicgraph.linkedin.com/content/dam/me/economicgraph/en-us/download/Job-Seeker-Checklist.pdf
https://omahadoor.com/blog/keep-amazon-deliveries-safe-from-porch-pirates-with-liftmaster-in-garage-delivery/
https://www.definitions.net/definition/Google
https://www.forbes.com/sites/gabrielleigh/2020/03/05/qatar-airways-revisit-is-this-still-the-best-business-class/
https://www.accenture.com/in-en/insights/strategy/ai-the-momentum-mindset
https://www.devteam.space/blog/10-best-ai-apps/
https://investorshub.advfn.com/boards/read_msg.aspx?message_id=145774084
https://boingboing.net/2019/10/23/746627.html
https://trustedpsychicmediums.com/angel-numbers/angel-number-1001-meaning/
http://app.leg.wa.gov/documents/billdocs/2015-16/Htm/Bill%20Reports/House/1645-S2.E%20HBR%20APH%2016.htm
https://www.coursehero.com/file/p7d2dhtt/There-will-also-be-an-increase-in-the-internal-communication-systems-telephone/
https://www.accenture.com/in-en/insights/artificial-intelligence/artificial-intelligence-explained-executives
https://hai.stanford.edu/research/ai-index-2019
https://www.analyticsinsight.net/understanding-artificial-intelligence-a-comprehensive-glossary-of-terms-and-definitions/
https://www.gartner.com/smarterwithgartner/gartner-predicts-the-future-of-ai-technologies/
https://aws.amazon.com/machine-learning

https://cloud.google.com/products/ai/building-blocks
https://www.javatpoint.com/application-of-ai
https://en.wikipedia.org/wiki/Applications_of_artificial_intelligence
https://wire19.com/ai-development-engines-platforms/
https://geekflare.com/ai-platforms/
https://geekflare.com/ai-platforms/
https://autome.me/4-ai-predictions-and-warnings-by-elon-musk/
https://www.smithsonianmag.com/innovation/artificial-intelligence-future-scenarios-180968403/
https://www.pewresearch.org/internet/2018/12/10/artificial-intelligence-and-the-future-of-humans/
https://data-flair.training/blogs/future-of-ai/
https://futureoflife.org/background/benefits-risks-of-artificial-intelligence/?cn-reloaded=1
https://hackr.io/blog/future-of-artificial-intelligence
https://autome.me/4-ai-predictions-and-warnings-by-elon-musk/
https://emerj.com/ai-sector-overviews/ai-agriculture-present-applications-impact/
https://s3.amazonaws.com/duolingo-papers/other/vesselinov-grego.duolingo12.pdf
https://www.forbes.com/sites/cognitiveworld/2019/07/12/ai-applications-in-education/#49b8998162a3
https://www.forbes.com/sites/cognitiveworld/2019/07/26/how-ai-can-transform-the-transportation-industry/#1ecb19e84964
https://www.prescouter.com/2017/12/ai-impact-transportation-industry/
https://www.pwc.com/gx/en/industries/healthcare/publications/ai-robotics-new-health/transforming-healthcare.html
https://builtin.com/artificial-intelligence/artificial-intelligence-healthcare
http://www.wired.co.uk/article/cancer-risk-ai-mammograms
https://www.cntraveler.com/story/caryn-seidman-becker-ceo-of-clear-on-never-needing-id-again
https://ncstatehea.wordpress.ncsu.edu/tag/internship/
https://www.coursehero.com/file/25562432/ACCT-CH-5-QUESTIONSdocx/
https://emerj.com/ai-sector-overviews/ai-agriculture-present-applications-impact/
https://www.wipro.com/en-IN/business-process/why-banks-need-artificial-intelligence/
https://builtin.com/artificial-intelligence/artificial-intelligence-healthcare
https://www.cxotoday.com/business-intelligence/artificial-intelligence-in-healthcare-to-touch-8-bn-by-2026/
https://www.pwc.com/gx/en/industries/healthcare/publications/ai-robotics-new-health/transforming-healthcare.html
https://geekflare.com/ai-platforms/
https://www.biospectrumasia.com/analysis/46/11384/robotics-and-ai-to-be-the-face-of-new-health.html
Lexalytics.   https://www.lexalytics.com/lexablog/ai-in-education-present-future-ethics
https://www.forbes.com/sites/bernardmarr/2018/07/25/how-is-ai-used-in-education-real-world-examples-of-today-and-a-peek-into-the-future/
https://www.forbes.com/sites/cognitiveworld/2019/07/12/ai-applications-in-education/

https://www.cio.com/article/3308996/making-magic-in-media-and-entertainment-with-artificial-intelligence.html
https://wire19.com/ai-development-engines-platforms/
https://www.independent.co.uk/news/science/stephen-hawking-transcendence-looks-at-the-implications-of-artificial-intelligence-but-are-we-taking-9313474.html
https://codete.com/blog/how-banks-can-leverage-voice-and-speech-recognition-technologies/
https://autome.me/4-ai-predictions-and-warnings-by-elon-musk/
https://www.motor1.com/news/139370/porsche-918-replacement-coming-2025/
https://www.reddit.com/r/AskScienceDiscussion/comments/8ii2ik/what_is_the_probability_that_artificial/
https://www.cnbc.com/2017/07/17/elon-musk-robots-will-be-able-to-do-everything-better-than-us.html
https://www.smithsonianmag.com/innovation/artificial-intelligence-future-scenarios-180968403/
https://www.forbes.com/sites/cognitiveworld/2019/07/26/how-ai-can-transform-the-transportation-industry/
https://herbertrsim.com/blockchain-artificial-intelligence-post-pandemic/
https://laflecha.net/how-will-robotics-change-our-lives-in-the-near-future/
http://www.impactlab.net/2019/04/11/what-will-our-society-look-like-when-artificial-intelligence-is-everywhere/
https://www.wipro.com/en-IN/business-process/why-banks-need-artificial-intelligence/
Sharma, Dr. Deepika (2018-08-12T22:58:59). Machine Learning for Beginners, Managers and Researchers: A precise approach of understanding the cutting edge technology
Finlay, Steven. Artificial Intelligence and Machine Learning for Business: A No-Nonsense Guide to Data Driven Technologies
Yao, Mariya. Applied Artificial Intelligence: A Handbook For Business Leaders
Lenahan, Brian. Artificial Intelligence: Foundations for Business Leaders and Consultants . Aquitaine Innovation Advisors

About the Author

Ajit K Jha is a passionate technology geek and a subject matter expert in Data Science, AI, and Digital Marketing. He has over 20 years of global experience in IT and Management. He has successfully managed and delivered large-scale enterprise projects for fortune 500 organizations like CITI Bank, Deutsche Bank, Capital One Bank, State Street, GE, Vodafone, etc. in regions like North America, Europe, and Asia-Pacific. His passion for Data Science and AI has led him to gain in-depth knowledge and understanding of process discovery, analysis, monitoring with predictive/prescriptive analytics, and business strategy management. His current assignment includes to create an entire knowledge-ware for one of the most renowned Data Science and Artificial Intelligence certification bodies in the world and as a subject-matter-expert solve all business queries for both the domains.

Ajit has a Master's degree in Computer Science and is an MBA from Indian Institute of Management, Lucknow (IIM Lucknow), India. He is also a certified Senior Data Scientist (SDS), SAS Certified Advanced Analytics Professional, and a Project Management Professional (PMP).

www.ingramcontent.com/pod-product-compliance
Lightning Source LLC
LaVergne TN
LVHW051320050326
832903LV00031B/3283